HARMON ZEIGLER, the author of this
book, is Associate Professor of Political Science and Research Associate, Center for the
Advanced Study of Educational Administration (Institute for Community Studies) at the
University of Oregon. Among his other publications are *Interest Groups in American
Society* and *Voting Patterns: A Local Election*; he has also been a frequent contributor
to *Public Opinion Quarterly, Journal of Politics,* and *American Political Science Review.*

THE
POLITICAL LIFE
OF AMERICAN
TEACHERS

Harmon Zeigler

PRENTICE-HALL, INC.

A SPECTRUM BOOK *Englewood Cliffs, New Jersey*

ACKNOWLEDGMENTS

I wish to acknowledge the generous financial assistance of the Center for the Advanced Study of Educational Administration, Institute for Community Studies, University of Oregon. A grant from this institution made it possible for me to take time off from teaching responsibilities in order to complete the research reported here. Roland Pellegrin, Director, and Philip Runkel, Associate Director, are responsible for providing an atmosphere in which it was possible to think and write with a minimum of distractions. I am also grateful to Professor Runkel for allowing me to interrupt him almost constantly throughout the writing of this book in order to benefit from his skill as a psychologist.

M. Kent Jennings of the University of Michigan provided a useful critique of portions of the manuscript, as did Patrick Mancy, then of the Oregon Education Association, now a staff member of the Committee on Education and Labor, United States House of Representatives. Edgar Litt of the University of Wisconsin at Milwaukee read the entire manuscript and offered numerous suggestions for improvement. During the preparation of preliminary drafts, Professor Keith Goldhammer of the University of Oregon was able to improve my understanding of the evidence, perhaps because of his wide experience in educational administration. At later stages,

Jack Dennis, Kent Jennings, Edgar Litt, Marshall Goldstein, Lee Anderson, James Guthrie, and Thomas R. Dye, all participants in a seminar on politics and education held at the University of Oregon in the summer of 1966, provided an evaluation of the final three chapters.

During the time devoted to the collection of the data, I was fortunate in having the services of Ira Rohter, now of the University of Wisconsin at Milwaukee, and Norman Luttbeg, now of Southern Illinois University. These two scholars came to Oregon from Michigan State University to spend a year in completing their dissertations and were invaluable in the planning of the study. During the later stages of writing and analysis, James Hutter, Richard Styskal, and Daniel Langmeyer filled the gap created by the departure of Rohter and Luttbeg. Michael Baer and Thom Lane assumed a major portion of the responsibilities for getting the material in and out of the computer.

I am especially indebted to James Murray and Peter Grenquist of Prentice-Hall for their encouragement and patience.

CONTENTS

Part Two

THE
POLITICAL LIFE
OF AMERICAN
TEACHERS

INTRODUCTION

This book seeks to describe the behavior of high school teachers *qua* teachers and then to attempt some generalizations about political behavior using teachers as examples. It is not possible to achieve an exact separation of the two levels of inquiry; they overlap continually, and no unit of discussion can be considered to exhaust a point of inquiry.

The description of teachers behavior is based on several interlocking strands of thought. First, it is assumed that the educational system can be understood as a subsystem of a general political system. This is hardly a novel or original conclusion.[1] However, when people write about political subsystems they usually include institutions the acts of which are so heavily laden with political consequences that the appellation *political* is the only alternative— political parties and political pressure groups, for instance, are clearly political institutions, but there are less clearly political institutions the acts of which have political consequences of a less immediate nature. I cannot conceive of an institution the acts of which are absolutely unrelated to the political system. I view the nature of a particular institution as resting somewhere along a continuum ranging from more political to less political, never just political or nonpolitical. Thus, the educational system has an orientation that is not primarily related to politics, and of all the consequences that flow from the activity of the educational system, political consequences may not be the most important. Yet it is certain that some of the acts of the educational system have implications for the political process.

The most obvious consequence is political socialization. As Easton and Hess, Key, Greenstein, and many others have suggested,

[1] See, for example, David Easton, "The Function of Formal Education in a Political System," *The School Review* (Autumn 1957), pp. 304-16.

1

children must be educated to perform the kinds of political roles expected of them.[2] Educational institutions are not the sole performers of this task; indeed, they may be subordinate to other agents, for instance the family. However, as Easton suggests, the mere fact that schools have access to the mind of a child for at least ten years during a period of critical development leads us to assume that the impact of schools on the political system is considerable.[3] Hess and Torney have recently supported Easton's belief. They found the school to be a major influence in the development of political attitudes among the young.[4]

Most of the current research on the subject of socialization is concerned with the effects of specific experiences (including educational experiences) upon the values and perceptions of youth, but this book is concerned with the behavior of *agents* of socialization. Teachers may not necessarily be influential within the power structure of the school considered as an organization, but it is they who are the vital cog in the educational subsystem for it is they who have the most direct and sustained interaction with students. It is the teacher who, whether deliberately or indirectly, suggests or emphasizes certain political values and avoids discussion of others. It is important, therefore, to know what teachers believe and to what extent they transmit their beliefs to students.

The transmission of material through the socialization process occurs by various modes. Mitchell, Easton and Hess, and others have categorized the various types of material which can be transmitted. Mitchell, for example, elucidates the following types of things which are taught: political motivation (the duty to participate), political values (individual freedom, equality, and so on), partisan values, political norms (fair play, being a good loser, and the like), and political information.[5] The values we examine in

[2] David Easton and Robert D. Hess, "Youth and the Political System," in Seymour M. Lipset and Leo Lowenthal, eds., *Culture and Social Character* (New York: The Free Press of Glencoe, Inc., 1961), pp. 226-51; V. O. Key, Jr., *Public Opinion and American Democracy* (New York: Alfred A. Knopf, 1961); Fred Greenstein, *Children and Politics* (New Haven: Yale University Press, 1965).

[3] Easton, *op. cit.*, p. 314.

[4] Reported in *The American Behavioral Scientist*, 9 (November 1965), p. 301.

[5] William C. Mitchell, *The American Polity* (New York: The Free Press of Glencoe, Inc., 1962), pp. 146-58.

this study fall somewhere between political values and partisan values. They are not so broad and consensual as freedom and equality, nor are they pinned to a specific reference group, such as a political party. Generally, the values can be understood as representing some dimension of liberalism or conservatism. We are attempting to describe the attitudes of teachers toward explicit problems of public policy—federal aid to education, for instance —and toward more general values, such as attitudes toward authority.

Teachers' overt expressions of their own political values are not the only ways that they may possibly influence students. They have to maintain discipline; therefore, it is not surprising that questions of authority are more immanent in their lives than they are in the lives of nonteachers. Problems of order and stability assume crucial importance. Consequently, we need to know whether or not the necessity of concern with the preservation of hierarchical relationships in the classroom predisposes the teacher toward a respect for established patterns of authority, irrespective of overt ideology.

Considered too is the extent to which the classroom is actually used as a forum for the discussion of political matters. High school teachers are encouraged to develop an enthusiasm for democracy among their students. Citizenship training does not, however, necessarily include the expression of explicit values concerning public policy alternatives. How does the teacher approach unsolved problems of public policy? Is the role of the teacher that of referee or advocate? How do teachers build up a perception of the proper role of the class? We assume that their perceptions of their role cannot be considered without first describing their perceptions of sanctions. Schools, perhaps because they have such extended access to the minds of youth, are constrained in their acts by societal expectations. The threat of sanctions may present the expression of an opinion which, all other things being equal, would have been expressed. Even though the teacher has an explicit value which he would like to convey to his students, he may elect not to do so for fear of the consequences. Thus, perceptions of environments are important aspects of the political role of the teacher.

Equally important are perceptions of from where the most severe sanctions might emanate. Of whom are teachers most afraid? Do they fear sources external to the school system, such as patriotic groups? Or do internal authorities, such as the principal, appear to be more persistent sanctioners? Perceptions of sanctioning sources are functions both of accurate appraisals of the real world and distortions resulting from the individual characteristics of the teacher. For example, beginning teachers may look at the same outside world in a way vastly different from the way their more experienced colleagues do.

We inquire into sanctions, then, and into defenses against sanctions. The relationship of the teacher to his professional organization is the place to begin. Like members of most other occupational categories, teachers have developed formal organizations to act as communicators between the individual and the external world. Such interest groups are supposed to mediate the individual with his environment by providing him with the influence of an organization through which to voice and hopefully to satisfy his political demands. Who participates in the organization, what the participants expect from the organization, the extent to which the participants are satisfied in their expectations, and the extent to which the organization modifies the behavior of the participants are relevant subjects for our inquiry.

The portion of the inquiry which is less relevant to understanding the role of educational institutions in the political system and more concerned with understanding a portion of general political behavior deals, not with what teachers think and how they express themselves, but rather with some possible explanations as to *why* they have certain values and adopt certain modes of expression. There are wide variations in teacher behavior depending upon a multitude of socio-economic characteristics. Social science traditionally considers race, class, party affiliation, occupation, education, income as the important independent variables to be used in the prediction of political outcomes such as voting or participation. Personality characteristics can be treated either as independent variables (i.e., authoritarian personalities are not in sympathy with the aspirations of minority groups) or as dependent variables (i.e., people with little formal education are more authoritarian than people with college educations).

The decision to concentrate upon one explanatory variable and to de-emphasize others was difficult to make. In this book, sex emerges as the single most important explanatory variable. The decision to orient the empirical sections around sex as a variable emerged as a means to some of the confusion developed as a result of reading discussions of the role of women in politics by Lane, Duverger, Campbell, Converse, Miller and Stokes, Greenstein, Terman and Tyler, and Helene Deutsch.[6] Most of these studies reached the same empirical conclusion: women are less active and less efficacious in the political process than men are. However, two different assumptions about the reasons for these differences emerge. On the one hand, differences are described as the result of social and cultural restraints imposed upon adult males and females. Presumably, economic and social modernization and the concomitant emancipation of women would reduce these differences, perhaps ultimately to the point of insignificance. On the other hand, there is evidence that differences in awareness of political events between the sexes are the result of inherent psychological differences. Greenstein found that sex differences appeared at a very early age and that "psychological underpinnings of political sex differences" might prevent changes in adult experiences and expectations from having a maximum impact.[7]

Presumably, such differences make it easy for women to accept role beliefs imposed upon them by society. Duverger and Campbell, Converse, Miller and Stokes note, for instance, that women are dependent upon men for political information. Duverger states that "while women have legally ceased to be minors, they still have the mentality of minors in many fields and, particularly in politics, they usually accept paternalism on the part of men. The

[6] Robert E. Lane, *Political Life* (New York: The Free Press of Glencoe, Inc., 1965); Maurice Duverger, *The Political Role of Women* (Paris: United Nations Economic, Social and Cultural Organization, 1955); Angus Campbell, Philip E. Converse, Warren E. Miller, and Donald E. Stokes, *The American Voter* (New York: John Wiley & Sons, Inc., 1960); Fred Greenstein, *op. cit.*; Lewis M. Terman and Leona Tyler, "Psychological Sex Differences," in Leonard Charmichael, ed., *Manual of Child Psychology* (2nd ed. New York: John Wiley & Sons, Inc., 1954), chapter 17; Helene Deutsch, *The Psychology of Women* (New York: Grune & Stratton, Inc., 1944).

[7] Greenstein, *op. cit.*, p. 127.

man—husband, fiancé, lover, or myth—is the mediator between them and the political world." [8]

What bothered me about these assumptions is that they seemed to rest upon the premise that women are best understood as home-makers and not breadwinners. What about women who make as much money as men within a given occupation, or to put it another way, what about men whose salaries are equalled by those of women? Studying teachers, one has an opportunity to observe the interaction of presumed psychological differences and societal roles. Even if society assigns to women a submissive political role, the teaching occupation enables them to develop a taste for the mas-culine world "making a living." But do male high school teachers, engaged as they are in a profession traditionally considered fem-inine, continue to assert the dominance ascribed to them either by society or by their psychological predispositions? Because of the unique nature of the teaching profession (it is one of the few that is open to men and women on an equal basis), the opportunity to study sex roles in politics seemed ideal.

Chapters I and II deal primarily with the recruitment, ideologies, and perceptions of teachers. Chapters III-V relate these personal characteristics to the behavior of teachers in the classroom, the professional organization, and the community.

The study is based upon interviews with 803 high school teach-ers living in Oregon. The sample is a stratified, random one in which the teaching population of medium and small towns was oversampled to provide a more equal distribution than would have occurred otherwise because of the heavy concentration of Oregon's population in metropolitan areas. It was feared that this might distort the proportion of men to women since we did not know whether either sex tended to concentrate in either metropolitan or small town schools. However, in the sample, the proportion of males is 60.5 per cent, which compares with 58.8 per cent in the actual population. The interviews were conducted by professional interviewers from January to March 1965. In order to maximize the generalizations based upon the data, information from com-parative sources is included whenever possible. In addition, during the planning of the study, it became possible for a portion of the

[8] Duverger, *op. cit.*, p. 129.

interview schedule to be administered by a smaller national sample of social studies teachers, in connection with a project being conducted by Professor Kent Jennings of the University of Michigan. An examination of the two sets of findings indicates that the attitudes of the Oregon teachers do not differ significantly from the national "control group." This is not to say, of course, that regional differences do not exist. In describing the far west, John Gillin has written that "Conformity for the individual is probably lowest of any region. . . . Far Westerners are perhaps less bound by Puritan consciences than residents of other regions." [9] As the reader will soon discover, these characteristics do not seem to be applicable to teachers, suggesting that the effect of regional culture is muted by the effect of occupation.

A more technical, and less general, summary of the research may be found in *The Political World of the High School Teacher* (University of Oregon, Center for the Advanced Study of Educational Administration, 1966). All information which is not documented is drawn from this source.

[9] John Hillin, "National and Regional Cultural Values in the United States," *Social Forces*, 34 (December, 1955), 113.

Part One

In this section particular attention is given to a recent phenomenon in educational history: the recruitment of large numbers of men into high school teaching. I am especially interested in the attitudes of male teachers in an environment which has traditionally been dominated by females. Starting from the assumptions of role theory, the central question is: What sorts of values and perceptions distinguish male teachers from their female counterparts? The essential argument is that the influx of males has not converted secondary school teaching into an essentially masculine enterprise. On the contrary, the evidence indicates that this influx has led, for a variety of reasons, to the playing of feminine roles by men. The roles which I have reference to are political roles. However, it is also the case that men approach the teaching career in a fashion fundamentally different than do women; and the differing expectations of the two sexes influence their perceptions and attitudes. The nature of the exploration, then, is the relationship between environmental conditions, roles, and attitudes.

Closely related to the role of men and women in teaching is the existence of different patterns of social mobility. The recruitment of males has taken place equally among all social strata of the society. It has long been assumed in the literature of educational sociology that teachers reinforce middle class values because they are products of this particular class. However, since high school teaching is not especially financially rewarding in comparison to other occupations which require similar educational attainment, males from middle and upper class families have not chosen this career. In contrast, women (who perceive teaching as a contingent rather than a dominant role) are still drawn from the middle and upper classes. Thus, differences based upon sex are compounded by differences based upon mobility.

The two basic factors, sex and mobility, are used to explain the attitudes of teachers toward the political world and the more immediate educational environment. Emphasis is placed both upon overt political ideology, measured in terms of the dimension of liberalism and conservatism, and upon perceptions of the political process, described by means of estimates of political alienation and cynicism. At this point, the concern of the book is with values, rather than behavior. It is assumed, however, that behavior is related (although not perfectly) with the attitudes to be described in this section.

Chapter One:
MALE AND FEMALE: DIFFERING PERCEPTIONS OF THE TEACHING EXPERIENCE

The differential roles of men and women in politics have not been studied very extensively, and among those studies which have been made the main focus is upon voting behaviors in elections. The general conclusions of these limited studies suggest quite strongly that men take a more active role in politics than do women. Explanations of this phenomenon center upon the concept of sexually differentiable roles. The argument is that the society assigns a dominant power-wielding role to men and a submissive receptive role to women.

No matter how one might want to quarrel about niceties of definition, politics is an arena for the exercise of power and control, and equation of the political role with the masculine role accordingly is not illogical. Yet, gross classification of political roles according to sex overlooks many of the subtleties of being a man or a woman. In political life, economic and social modernization is gradually eroding sex differences in political roles, but this does not mean that popular perceptions of masculine and feminine roles have changed. For instance, if the popular stereotype defines the masculine role as one of power and dominance, what can we say of men who hold an occupation that is perceived as feminine?

THE FEMINIZATION OF THE TEACHING ROLE

Secondary school teachers, males not less than females, are playing just such a feminine role. At the elementary level, teaching is almost exclusively a woman's occupation; in higher education, men predominate. At the secondary level, however, there is a relatively

11

even balance of male and female teachers. About two out of three male teachers are in high schools, and at the high school level today males are a slight majority of the teaching population. This numerical balance of the sexes, however, does not diminish the primarily female dominance of the educational establishment.

The numerical dominance of males in high school teaching is relatively new. In 1950 males made up only about 40 per cent of the high school teaching population; by 1960 males made up the majority. The rapid increase in the male teaching population at the high school level is the result of elaborate inducements offered both in colleges of education and in public schools to diminish female dominance of the teaching profession. The reasons for these efforts are not based on an assumption that men are better teachers than women; rather, they stem from the concept of authority.

The teacher's first task in the classroom is to establish authority over the pupils. Educational psychologists believe that the child's need to identify with a father figure offers a good way through which to establish the teacher's classroom authority and to improve the pupil's learning experience. The identification problems of girls are not very severe. However, if a boy establishes an emotional contact primarily with women teachers, it is believed the school can offer him little help in learning a male role, for women represent the values of mothers and homemakers and can hardly be expected to provide male guidelines. So the effort to recruit males was begun, and it has been successful. However, I maintain that, far from converting the secondary school establishment from a feminine into a masculine enterprise, the recruitment of male teachers into secondary teaching has led to the playing of a feminine role by men.

It must be clearly understood that by *feminine role* I do not mean an *effete role*. I mean, rather, that laymen *look upon* teaching traditionally as a woman's job; insofar as high school teaching is thus interpreted to be a feminine role, those who play that role conform to society's expectations for it; and that it is consequently difficult for a male teacher to establish male authority in this role. I further intend to argue that males who play this feminine role behave politically much as do women, although it cannot be argued that they do this solely *because* they are high school teachers.

The feminization of teaching is primarily an American phenomenon. In most other countries men have always assumed a major role in secondary education. Richard Hofstadter has succinctly described the position of the male teacher in America:

> But in America, *where teaching has been identified as a feminine profession, it does not offer men the stature of a fully legitimate male role.* The American masculine conviction that education and culture are feminine concerns is thus confirmed, and no doubt partly shaped, by the experiences of boys in school. . . . The boys grow up thinking of men teachers as somewhat effeminate and treat them with a curious mixture of genteel deference (of the sort due to women) and hearty male condescension. In a certain constricted sense, the male teacher may be respected, but he is not "one of the boys." [1]

Most of the formal teachers' organizations do not provide for separate organizations for high school teachers. Consequently, assuming an equal attendance at professional meetings by elementary and high school teachers, male teachers are still outnumbered by female teachers. Even more important, it takes a long time for popular stereotypes to be erased. Males now comprise the majority of the high school teaching population, but the image of the schoolmarm still plagues them. In 1932, Willard Waller published a book that has since become a classic, *The Sociology of Teaching.*[2] In an anecdote about a high school principal's experience in a barbershop, Waller describes the stereotypic treatment of teachers. As the man enters, the barber, who apparently has been telling off-color stories, hushes his clients. Recognizing the artificiality of the situation, the principal encourages resumption of normal conversation, but to no avail. After the principal leaves the shop the conversation resumes, but the barber admonishes his clients to be on their guard whenever a teacher or principal enters because, he says, "I have many women customers." As Waller comments:

---

[1] Richard Hofstadter, *Anti-Intellectualism in American Life* (New York: Vintage Books, 1963), p. 320. Italics supplied. See also Margaret Mead, *The School in American Culture* (Cambridge: Harvard University Press, 1951), pp. 5-6.

[2] New York: John Wiley & Sons, Inc., 1965. Recently reissued in paperback, this book has been widely used in courses dealing with the sociology of education.

The assimilation of the teachers of the feminine character ideal, the suppression of normal activity when the teacher entered the room— all these things make the above stand out as an interesting and significant incident. It has been said that no woman and no Negro is ever fully admitted to the white man's world. Possibly we should add men teachers to the list of the excluded.[3]

I have discussed Waller's decades-old comments with many educators, and most of them believe that the situation is still much the same today. High school teachers throughout the country are sensitive to the fact that the pronoun *she* is almost invariably used in discussions about teachers and most of the literature about teachers uses this pronoun. In a Supreme Court decision [Adler v. Board of Education, 342 U.S. 485 (1952)] involving plaintiffs all of whom were made high school teachers, the opinion handed down by the Court uses the pronoun *she*. Recruitment of males into the high school teaching population did not really get started until the middle 1950's, long after most of the adults in today's society were high school students. It is perhaps only natural, then, that when people think back upon a high school teacher, they think in terms of *her*.

It may well be that the tenacity of the stereotype will be reduced in a few generations, Teachers and administrators certainly hope so. A popular series of TV dramas, "Mr. Novak," produced with the approval of the National Education Association, is a clear example of the vigorous efforts being made to change the stereotype.[4] However, sociologists have learned that stereotypes are not accurate reflections of reality and that stereotypes persist long after their counterpart realities have changed, or disappeared. For example, an occupation that, like high school teaching, is burdened with the stereotype problem is that of the lobbyist. Popular press exposés condemn lobbyists as subverters of the public interest.

---

[3] *Ibid.,* p. 50.

[4] In spite of the fact that this program's hero was a male high school teacher, male teachers had a less positive reaction to the program than did female teachers. In a survey of teachers, conducted by the National Education Association, 60 per cent of the female teachers but only 49 per cent of the male teachers who viewed "Mr. Novak" felt that the program had a good effect on their own morale and self-esteem. Perhaps this result is related to the fact that fewer male than female teachers believed that the dramatizations were reasonable portrayals of the real problems of real high school teachers.

Lobbyists, supposed to be the evil power behind the scenes, the manipulators of practically all legislative decisions, are often depicted as smoking long, black cigars while lavishly distributing money in an attempt to buy the vote of legislators. In fact, lobbyists, at least those who make lobbying a full-time career, are generally well-educated advocates of a particular point of view and spend most of their time transmitting information, not money, to legislators. Most legislators regard lobbyists as very useful in the legislative process precisely because lobbyists can provide information that might not otherwise be readily available. It is probably true, especially at the state level, that at one time lobbyists did engage in corrupt practices. Today lobbyists are trying desperately to live down this stereotyped image and are extremely sensitive to public criticism. Many are reluctant to be called lobbyists, preferring to be known as *legislative representatives* or some other such innocuous term.

Male high school teachers, like lobbyists, are struggling to overcome a stereotype. Doing what is popularly regarded as women's work has both tangible and relatively intangible consequences for male teachers. They not only suffer degradation of status by working in a feminine occupation, they also incur considerable degradation of financial rewards. Financial discrimination against male teachers exists relative to males in other occupations and relative to female teachers. It is true that male and female teachers are paid according to the same salary scales (it is also true that various under-the-table inducements are made to male teachers). However, the salaries of most married female teachers merely augment the husbands' income, whereas married male teachers must use the entirety of their salary to support their families. Female high school teachers are better paid than are most women working at other jobs. This is decidedly not the case with male teachers. Thus, not only are male teachers doing women's work, they are only getting paid women's wages for doing it. Men who become high school teachers may not expect to make as much money as they might were they to enter another occupation, it is nonetheless damage to the male ego for a man to be on a financial par with women. In practically every other occupation, the financial discrimination is against women. The failure of high school teaching to follow suit clearly makes the position of the male teacher somewhat unique.

Another way of analyzing the male and female roles in high school teaching is to examine the differing career orientations of the sexes. For both men and women, teaching is an unstable occupation, a contingent role rather than a dominant one. The turnover rate in high school teaching is exceptionally high. The reasons for this instability differ markedly as between men and women, however. Female teachers intend to teach only until they get married or until a bit later when they begin a family. The female perception of the teaching occupation is thus *in and out*. For males, however, the orientation is *up or out*. Males regard high school teaching as women's work, a stepping stone into either educational administration, which is almost entirely dominated by males, or into another profession altogether. Here is one of the frustrations of the male high school teacher: only about a third of the male beginning teachers anticipate remaining in that occupation until retirement, yet in actual practice, more males than females remain career teachers.

Insofar as teaching is a feminized occupation, and if it is assumed that teaching is a middle-class occupation, then for males teaching becomes a mechanism of status change while for females it is a mechanism of status maintenance. The majority of males who become high school teachers come from lower-class backgrounds, whereas the majority of females who become high school teachers come from middle- and upper-class backgrounds. For males entering teaching, then, a change in status comes about as they move up into a subsystem with a female ethos. Significantly, women rank public school teaching substantially higher in occupational status than men do.

Robert Lane observed that "A person's work life is certain to color his outlook on society, to structure his attitudes, and to affect his behavior." [5] This is to say that it is not necessarily a person's occupation as such but rather his perception of his occupation that colors his attitudes. To some persons, occupation is clearly a major component of personal identity, but others look upon occupation in a much more casual fashion, viewing it primarily as a

[5] Robert Lane, *Political Life* (New York: The Free Press of Glencoe, Inc., 1965), p. 331.

money-making device that is not a major determinant of one's total life style. Teaching appears less likely to elicit total commitment than other professions, hence it might be expected that the teaching experience would not operate to produce in the teacher a cohesive set of values. Actually, different types of people react to the teaching experience in different ways, but there is evidence that the teaching experience does operate to amalgamate the need structures of varying types of people to produce a pattern common to all teaching groups. There is also evidence suggesting that the teaching experience molds a characteristic set of personality traits. To illustrate, a person has many identities. In addition to such given identities as sex and race, one is further identified by his occupation, income, education, place of residence, and so forth. Consider the forces at work in the Southern judge striving to teach a decision on a question of racial integration. Will he react primarily as a Southerner reared in the traditions of segregation, or as a judge required by law and the judicial tradition to enforce impartially the decisions of the legislature or a higher court?

The way a person will react in a decision-making situation depends upon the relative strengths of the identities at work in him. It is questionable that one can talk about teachers as a whole on the assumption that personality variables are eroded by the teaching experience. It is the argument of this book that the teaching experience has greatly diverse impacts upon recruits into the profession according to what combination of personality and social variables each recruit brings into the teaching career, but that the basic variable—hence the key to understanding individual reactions to the teaching career—is sex. In short, men teachers and women teachers are different animals, and the remarkable political behavior of men teachers can be understood as a masculine reaction to their feminine occupational role.

WHAT TEACHING DOES TO TEACHERS

Waller has described the teacher as being inflexible, conservative, and as having an abnormal concern about status. Waller believes that if one does not have these traits when he starts teaching, he develops them before long.[6] His argument is that these traits flow

[6] Waller, pp. 386-400.

naturally out of the relations of teachers with their students: The first order of business on the agenda of the high school teacher is to establish who is boss. The teacher must define the teacher-student situation for the students: discipline must be maintained. For the male high school teacher, paradoxically, this can be difficult, although the argument in favor of recruitment of more males into the teaching profession rests upon the assumption that males can impose authority more easily and can readily establish a father image (at least for male students). The method of establishing authority most frequently relied on by teachers involves performance of some rather dramatic act during the first session of a class. For example, a teacher is usually able to locate the one or two students in the class who are most likely to lead a minor revolt, primarily because they are looked upon by the other students as leaders. Having located the potential troublemakers, the teacher's task is to put them in their place. This confrontation occasionally takes the form of actual physical combat. In a sense, then, the teacher is acting somewhat like an officer in the Army but without the status or sanctioning power available to an officer. The maintenance of the superordinate-subordinate relationship leads to personal rigidity, and the teacher's dominant need, based upon fear of loss of authority, is for security. Hence, security is exaggerated in the need structure of teachers in comparison to other values. Whether the characteristics of conservatism, rigidity, and the need for security that teachers display are personality characteristics which influence one to choose teaching rather than some riskier calling or whether these characteristics are a product of teaching has not been established. Rogers's view that "It is likely that the people who enter the teaching profession *are* conservative . . . because individualists fear the regimentation imposed on teachers . . ." is provocative but speculative.[7] The portrait of the teacher nonetheless is of one who is not likely to do unconventional things or to engage in unconventional behavior. It is my belief, however, that as a portrait of the teacher, it is far more one of the male than of the female teacher. To advance this argument, let us examine the relative impacts that three variables—sex, income, and teaching ex-

[7] Dorothy Rogers, "Implications of Views Concerning the 'Typical' School Teacher," *Journal of Educational Sociology*, 59 (September 1953) 484.

perience—may have upon teacher behaviors and attitudes. There are three possible relationships among the three variables: first, males and females may have largely different characteristics of income and teaching experience; second, people at a given income level may have different characteristics irrespective of teaching experience and sex; and third, the teaching experience may operate to minimize differences based upon income or sex. If the third relationship proves true, then we may conclude that teaching is a role overwhelming male-female role differentials.

Let us see how sex, income, and teaching experience mold certain factors that may be presumed to be central to the life style of the individual. The factors are:

1. Job satisfaction,
2. Political values,
3. Educational values, and
4. Personal orientations toward life.

JOB SATISFACTION

Research has produced clear and unequivocal evidence indicating there is substantial job dissatisfaction among male teachers.[8]

One measure of a person's job satisfaction is whether or not he would choose the same occupation were he given the opportunity to start life over again. A substantial majority of the female teachers polled said they would choose teaching again, whereas only about one third of the male teachers indicated that they would again choose to become teachers. Males begin teaching with the expectation of moving up to a different, better job. What happens when these expectations are shattered? Money is important for males in our society, which measures success by material yardsticks, but do males with high incomes exhibit more satisfaction with their jobs than males with low incomes, or does it really matter? Is making a fairly high income a satisfactory compensation for doing women's work, or is good pay a poor reward for such denigration?

[8] Ward S. Mason, *The Beginning Teacher: Status and Career Orientations* (Washington: U.S. Department of Health, Education, and Welfare, 1961), pp. 81-83; National Education Association, *The American Public School Teacher, 1960-1961* (Washington: National Education Association, 1963), p. 67; National Education Association *Research Bulletin*, 35 (1957), p. 38.

Among low-income teachers (those with an annual family income of less than $10,000) about one third of the males are satisfied, compared to more than half the females. For teachers in this group an increase in teaching experience makes neither males nor females either more or less satisfied with their positions. In other words, the attitudes which they brought into the profession remain unchanged by the teaching experience. By contrast, the male teacher starting his career at a high income level is considerably more satisfied than his low-income counterpart. Thus, at least among *beginning male* teachers, money seems to be conducive to job satisfaction. Curiously enough, relatively inexperienced low-income female teachers are no less satisfied with their jobs than are relatively inexperienced high-income female teachers. The male who started out relatively satisfied and happy becomes dissatisfied. Presumably his dreams of moving on to a better job have been shattered and he is left with the unpleasant task of facing the truth: he has been teaching for years, he is not an administrator, he has not left teaching; he has been treading water. There is a decline in the job satisfaction of high-income males down to the point where, at the more experienced level, all males (irrespective of income) have roughly the same extent of satisfaction with their jobs. For females, a remarkably dissimilar pattern develops. For them, the cumulative effects of increasing income and increasing teaching experience operate to increase dramatically their satisfaction. What this means is that the teaching experience is beneficial to the job satisfaction of females, but is harmful for males.

It seems reasonable to suppose that financial reward is a basic ingredient in inducing job satisfaction. Why is this not the case among male high school teachers? The answer is simple. Relative to other occupations requiring similar education, male teachers are underpaid; perhaps more important, they receive the same compensation as female teachers. In every school district in the country school boards are gradually raising the salaries of teachers, under considerable pressure from educational associations and, occasionally, the threat of teacher walkouts. However, teaching is an occupation to which men and women have equal access, and it therefore may be that a basic cause of dissatisfaction among men may never be corrected. That is to say, no matter how high teacher salaries go, as long as men and women are paid equally job dissatisfaction among men teachers will not be reduced. The obvious if unconventional remedy for improving the self-esteem of the male teacher, then, is to introduce some sort of male-female salary scale differential. In an informal way this is already being done in many school districts. Increments to salaries can be earned for various extraclass duties, such as serving as advisor for student organizations, coaching, and supervision of extracurricular student affairs. The practice is to make these opportunities more available to men than to women.

POLITICAL CONSERVATISM

Citizens who concern themselves with public education often are anxious about how teacher values may affect the nature of the curriculum, and, through personal contacts, the students. Seeking to categorize the political values of teachers, laymen usually describe a teacher as holding either liberal or conservative beliefs. Indeed, in the literature about teacher politics these words occur time and time again, although there is rarely any accompanying clear definition of *liberal* and *conservative* mean. Conservatism is a difficult idea to define with objectivity, and opinion polls are not necessarily the most reliable guide to a definition of conservatism in terms of overt ideology. An instrument called the Domestic Conservatism Scale, developed by political scientists, is an interesting attempt to establish a standard of conservatism by measuring individuals' attitudes toward such government activities as federal aid to education, integration of public schools, equalization of job opportunities, medical care for the aged, and so forth.[9] To educational sociologists, teachers appear to be conservative in the sense of being creatures of habit, not experimentalists by professional nature. The conservatism apparent in teachers is best understood, perhaps, by considering them as advocates of the interests of the middle class. Teachers prefer to do regular rather than radical things, and they do not encourage their students to participate in politics other than in the most accepted and established fashions. This interpretation is based upon the assumption that teachers,

[9] V. O. Key, Jr., *Public Opinion and American Democracy* (New York: Alfred A. Knopf, 1961), p. 561.

charged with the responsibility of injecting system maintenance values into the educational subculture, encourage their students to become good citizens and in so doing do not offer students an alternative to acceptance of the *status quo.*

For our purposes, *conservatism* is perhaps best defined as a personal reluctance to take risks, an inclination to and dependence upon the established order and patterns of behavior. Conservatism thus defined is an expression of middle-class values. In terms of this definition, teachers themselves think they are conservative, to judge by a recent National Education Association[10] poll of high school teachers in which 56 per cent of those who responded to a question asking them to classify themselves as either liberal or conservative chose the conservative alternative. Several findings of the NEA study are of relevance to our inquiry. The responses indicated that an overwhelming majority of teachers regard themselves as moderate conservatives or liberals; only about one fourth of the sample described themselves as ultraconservative or ultraliberal. Most of the moderates, however, lean toward the conservative end of the spectrum. Also of significance is the finding that about one third of the women but almost one half of the men indicated that they regard themselves as liberals. It is, of course, generally true that women, irrespective of occupation, are considered somewhat more conservative than men, and so this finding is not surprising.

Conservatism is often equated with conformity to middle-class values. Beyond question, it is a difficult matter to establish exactly what middle-class values are, even more difficult to measure them. In the literature that attempts to catalog the presumed values of the middle class, however, thrift, frugality, individual initiative, self-reliance, hard work, and respect for authority seem to occur most frequently.

There is yet another yardstick of conservatism, one that has become very much a part of the American vocabulary since the end of World War II. This archconservatism emphasizes morality and patriotism as its chief values. People who subscribe to this philos-

---

[10] National Education Association, *What Teachers Think: A Summary of Teacher Opinion Poll Findings, 1960-1965* (Washington: National Education Association, 1965), p. 51.

ophy avow profound love of country. They believe, for example, that American history should be taught so as to instill within the child a love of country. They believe they have discovered a fundamental breakdown in moral standards in this country (which perhaps can be traced to a decline in the acceptance of middle-class values). They argue that most of the basic evils of modern American society would be eradicated if Americans would return to something called old-fashioned patriotism. One intuitively suspects that all three interpretations of conservatism are somehow related, but it is possible that people who appear to be conservatives in their current postures on domestic public policy might not turn out to be conservatives if their attitudes were measured against middle-class values or archconservative dogmas.

Older people tend to be more conservative than younger people. Teachers become *more* conservative as their teaching experience increases. Is this tendency of teachers to become more conservative a specific function of the teaching experience, or is it a general function of the aging process? The answer to this is that among teachers of the same age those who have taught the longest tend to be the most conservative. What effect does the teaching experience have on the viability of middle-class values among teachers? Does teaching shape teachers into loyal volunteers of the middle-class, faithful advocates of the *status quo*, stern repressors of radicalism? Is this kind of conservatism more characteristic of female teachers than of male teachers? The evidence strongly suggests that teachers' allegiance to middle class values increases with teaching experience. It appears, however, that there is no relationship between age and allegiance to middle class values. Why is it that the teaching experience boosts the stock of the *status quo?* Is it because of community pressures demanding conformity from teachers? Is it because of teacher *perception* of community pressures demanding conformity? Or is it a consequence of teachers' desire to avoid threats to authority in the classroom? Children with strongly imbued middle-class values are likely to be well-behaved in the classroom.

There is a curious ambivalence attaching to the role of education as a transmitter of the values of culture. In schools of education the future teacher is taught that it is the job of the schools to build good democratic citizens. Accordingly, it is taught, students should be encouraged to express themselves to the end of developing in them a healthy interest in participating in the affairs of society, and the best forum for such expression is within the school itself. But there is the problem of discipline: student activism must not disrupt the smooth flow of the classroom situation. Sociologists of education maintain that the classroom authority of the teacher is slipping and that respect for teachers is diminishing among students. It is therefore quite possible that the necessity for maintaining discipline overrides the textbook obligation of teachers to encourage student self-expression.

Teachers' allegiance to middle-class values increases with teaching experience, but among low-income teachers (irrespective of sex) that allegiance becomes extremely tenacious. When asked about their experiences with the maintenance of proper discipline, the majority of teachers responding to the NEA study answered that maintaining classroom discipline had become progressively more difficult than it was when they first started teaching, and the longer the experience the greater the perceived increase in the difficulty of maintaining discipline. Only about one fourth of the relatively inexperienced teachers but a majority of the more experienced teachers, claimed that discipline seemed to be increasingly difficult to maintain.

It appears that the high-income female teachers, who are politically conservative, have very low allegiance to middle-class values. Male teachers, on the other hand, even those who are political liberals, demonstrate high allegiance to middle-class values in comparison with women. These findings may relate to the fact that maintaining discipline is much more of a problem for male teachers than for female teachers; indeed, one suspects that the crisis in authority is related to the recruitment of male teachers. Male teachers tend to seek out the comfort and security of a disciplined, middle-class conformist world. Paradoxically, however, the recruitment of males into the high school teaching profession has brought male teachers into the majority, but has not brought about the concomitant learning situation that one would expect. It appears that the mere existence of males does not automatically produce discipline, perhaps because the desired creation of a strongly masculine figure has not occurred.[11]

My-country-right-or-wrong conservatism, the radical right, which received an enthusiastic if somewhat unclear articulation by the Republican Party in the 1964 Presidential election, seems to appeal less to female teachers than to male teachers, especially to those making low income relative to length of teaching experience. Among such males, the longer their teaching experience the more conservative they tend to be. There are probably more moderate than radical conservatives among the teaching population.

Conservatism among male teachers seems to be related to the fact that most male teachers do not like their work. It appears that one method of creating an advocate of the Radical Right is to take a male, place him in the incongruously feminine teaching role, keep him there for years and at low income, and allow his hopes for advancement to fade as his experience increases but his situation does not change. Male teachers are a disadvantaged segment, and their attitudes reflect a correlation between job satisfaction and conservatism. By contrast, the moderate conservatism typically espoused by female teachers, on the other hand, seems to be essentially the traditional conservatism of the middle and upper classes, a conservatism which reflects, not anxiety, but rather an essential satisfaction with one's society and his or her position in it.

ATTITUDES TOWARD EDUCATION: A PROGRESSIVE ORTHODOXY?

Conservatism, whatever its mode of expression, bespeaks a disposition to maintain things as they are. If it is true that teaching tends to confirm teachers in political conservatism, it is therefore reasonable to suppose that the teaching experience tends to confirm them in educational conservatism also. Educational conservatives are those who do not like progressive education. Whereas the roots of the political conservatism of the high school teacher are somewhat ambiguous, the educational establishment, as it is represented in schools of education, vigorously fosters the cause of educational

[11] Leo J. Cronbach, *Educational Psychology* (New York: Harcourt, Brace and Co., 1954), p. 318.

progressivism. Progressivism is the establishment's orthodoxy. Certainly the recent attacks upon American education, critical of the emphasis on techniques rather than subject matter, whether or not one agrees with them, have correctly described the dominant theme of the training of public secondary school teachers. An occasional revolt, principally in the form of public candidates running for the school board on a platform of returning to the three R's, does not diminish very much the firm control that educational progressives have over the training of public school teachers. Progressive teachers would prefer to abandon the traditional discipline and learning that had little regard for individual needs, and to substitute for them a program in which the student is in essence allowed to set his own pace. One envisions a confrontation, for example, between teachers who prefer to return to the practice of administering a good spanking when other methods fail and teachers who would like to see psychiatric services made available in the public schools from kindergarten up.

These comments about the orthodoxy of educational progressivism are offered primarily to prepare the reader for the finding that, unlike political conservatism, educational conservatism *decreases* with teaching experience. As teachers are becoming politically more conservative, they are simultaneously becoming educationally more progressive. Moderate political conservatism and educational progressivism are values which conform to the expectations of the educational system, and are values which are held by those who have derived the most benefits from the system. On the other hand, radical conservatism and lack of belief in the methods of progressive education are deviant attitudes held by those who have derived the least benefit from the system. The pattern of conformity is typical of females; the pattern of deviance is typical of males. For example, high-income females, politically the most conservative, are educationally the most progressive. It is hardly coincidental that teachers in this group are also the most satisfied with their jobs and hence can be assumed to be deriving the most psychological benefits from the educational system.

Corroborative evidence is provided by the NEA survey, which showed that about 60 per cent of the male high school teachers would use physical punishment as a disciplinary measure, as compared to about 40 per cent of the female high school teachers. Approximately 25 per cent of the female teachers but only about 13 per cent of the male teachers reported that they never have any disciplinary problems, which perhaps explains the greater readiness of the men to resort to physical punishment.[12]

The real problem here is, not the disposition of males to radical conservatism and lack of educational progressivism, but that these attitudes may be related to the crisis of authority, a situation that in turn can be related to the incursion of men into what had been almost exclusively a feminine occupation. That male teachers should develop antiestablishment attitudes is understandable, but has resulted in high schools staffed with teachers who do not like their work, who espouse an ideology of discontent, and who reject the educational orthodoxy of the educational establishment. Whether one judges this to be good or bad depends entirely upon his own values. One might predict that this dissident element would ultimately become absorbed and conform. This is the established pattern of deviant movements in the political world. On the other hand, the extent to which males are able to increase their benefits from the educational system and reduce their nonconformity depends, paradoxically, less upon the educational system itself than upon the general society. For male teachers to become more satisfied with their jobs, they will first have to be accorded more legitimacy by society itself.

PERSONAL RIGIDITY

The position of the male teacher should become especially perilous in the classroom, for it is the classroom that provides the greatest threat to a teacher's authority. The classroom situation is supposed to contribute to the development of an unusually high concern with status and authority among teachers. Facing a crisis of authority, teachers can be expected to emphasize superior-subordinate relationships and to be suspicious of change, for they prefer that their professional world be structured so as to minimize risk-taking and to maximize established authority.

Two indices—tolerance of change and need for respect—of these

[12] National Education Association, *Student Behavior in Secondary Schools,* 1964 (NEA, August, 1965).

dimensions of personality were used in the Oregon study. The expectation was that these measures would discriminate distinctive male-female attitude differences. The tolerance-of-change index measured the willingness of individuals to try something new without prior knowledge of the consequences. Those willing to accept change are, in a sense, risk-takers. Those unwilling to accept change are typified by the person who fits himself into a routine and sticks to it, who prefers the security of established procedures to the insecurity of new ideas.

Teachers are presumed to have a high need for respect. The use in the Oregon study of an index to measure these dimensions of teacher personality rests largely upon the theoretical contributions of Waller, who observed that:

> Inflexibility or unbendingness of personality, which we have mentioned as characterizing the school teacher, flows naturally out of his relations with his students. The teacher must maintain a constant pose in the presence of students. . . . The teacher must not accept the definition of situations which students work out but must impose his own definition upon the students. . . . The teacher lives much by the authority role. . . . Those who live by one role must learn to defend its ultimate implications. . . . On the objective side, this dignity which arises in the classroom is an exaggerated concern over all the ramifications of respect and the formal amenities due to one who occupies a narrow but well-defined social status. . . . In the life of every teacher there is significant long-term change in the psychic weight of these roles, a not unusual result being that role number one, the authority role, eats up the friendly role or absorbs so much of the personality that nothing is left for friendliness to fatten upon.[13]

Waller made these observations at a time when two-thirds of the nation's high school teachers were women. It now appears, however, that the syndrome he observed—rigid personality, exaggerated concern for authority, and a deep need for respect—is more pronouncedly characteristic of male teachers than of female teachers. Male teachers are substantially more routinized than female teachers. This relationship is especially pronounced among high-income teachers. Nearly 60 per cent of the high-income female teachers are *not* opposed to change, whereas nearly 60 per cent of the males in

[13] Waller, *op. cit.*, pp. 386-400.

this category *are* opposed to change. If as Waller suggests the classroom situation produces a deep need for respect, then those who have the most experience in the classroom should have the deepest need for respect. But experienced teachers demonstrated no greater need for respect than did less experienced teachers, even though the more experienced teachers indicated that the maintenance of classroom discipline was a major problem, whereas the less experienced teachers indicated it was not. It develops, however, that the teaching experience produces a differential need for respect upon male and female teachers: men have a higher need for respect than women do. The differential reaches its most extreme proportions among the higher income groups, where about 30 per cent of the male teachers have a depth of need for respect that is equalled by only about 15 per cent of the female teachers. Just as the job satisfaction of the male teacher does not depend solely upon income, neither does his need for respect. Low income males and high income males have about the same depth of need for respect.

The deep need for respect felt by males suggests that the teaching experience threatens their authority, for the respect accorded a teacher is a gauge of his authority. Women do not seem to have as great a concern for authority when they begin teaching and apparently are not as bothered by challenges to authority as men are. It is not just being a high school teacher that contributes to an exaggerated concern for authority, it is being a *male* teacher. The fact that male teachers have more trouble than women do in maintaining classroom discipline feeds this need for respect. An unusual paradox of status may be developing: as men they should be able to command respect, but apparently they cannot.

EMERGENT PATTERNS IN MALE
AND FEMALE VALUES

This chapter undertook to discover if male and female teachers react to the teaching experience in markedly different patterns. The evidence is that they do, and that the patterns are typified in the behaviors respectively of high-income females and low-income males. The high-income females have the greater satisfaction with their jobs, the lesser need for respect, the lesser opposition to change, the more conservative political opinions, not the lesser tendency to radical conservatism. They are also the more educationally progressive. The low income males are the less satisfied with their jobs, have the greater need for respect, and are more likely to oppose change. They are more liberal politically than females, but the most radically conservative of teachers are in this group. They are less educationally progressive than women.

Between these two extreme patterns fall the behavior of high-income males, who seem to have more in common with low-income males than with high-income females, and of low-income females, whose values seem at times closer to low-income males and at other times closer to high-income females. That is to say, for male teachers the clearest congruence of values is with those of other males, whereas females have a less exclusive tendency to adopt the values of other females. Granted that income is important for the males, it does not seem to provide a set of identifications as viable and permanent as simply being a male. Maleness emerges as the essential variable and the male high school teacher is, in a sense, the underclass of the teaching profession, a rebel in a female system.

Chapter Two:
VERTICAL MOBILITY
AND
POLITICAL PERCEPTIONS

Political scientists have written a great deal about the social class and voters, educational sociologists have written much about the social class and teachers. The bases of this outpouring lie in the assumptions of early sociological theory, which stressed the importance of social stratification. Early voting studies, reflecting this tradition, generally concluded that social class, religion, and so forth crucially affected the party loyalties of voters. However, political scientists gradually abandoned the beliefs that knowledge of a person's social class was the key to a knowledge of his political behavior and attitudes. In a sense, the disenchantment of political scientists with the importance of social class represents a disenchantment with traditional sociological theory. Indeed, part of the conflict between these two professions has come about because political scientists object to what they believe to be the obsession of sociologists with theories of social class and stratification.

This chapter will probably fan the flames of the controversy because it seems apparent that, while political scientists are looking for less static concepts as explanations of behavior, educational sociologists are still telling us that teachers, because they are themselves members of the middle class, are representative of middle class values. The notion that high school teachers, because of their class origins, buttress the position of the middle class in the society is a theme running through most of the literature on social stratification. This implication is especially strong in some of the early studies of the social origins of teachers. These studies, made at a time when high school teaching was still dominated by women, observed that recruits to the teaching profession came from middle- and upper-class families and tended to exaggerate middle-class ideologies and to avoid lower-class ideologies. Thus the recruitment pattern of the teaching profession was related to the contribution of the educational system to the maintenance of societal values. Lacking representatives of the lower classes, schools could hardly be expected to present alternatives to middle class ideologies.

THE CLASS ORIGINS OF TEACHERS

The argument that the key to the understanding of teacher behavior rests in the concept of social class will have to be re-examined because of the recruitment of males into the profession. In a society such as ours, with its strong emphasis on financial success, what social stratum is the most plausible hunting ground for new recruits into an occupation that is dominated by women, that offers relatively little hope of great financial reward, that enjoys only slightly above-average prestige? The answer is obvious: the drive to recruit males into the teaching population has been most successful among the lower classes. In the current teaching population, the majority of males have lower-class backgrounds while the majority of females have middle- and upper-class backgrounds. There is also some evidence that boys planning careers in education come from lower occupational backgrounds than do girls making similar plans.

Given the fact that the society requires that the male play the role of breadwinner, it is hardly surprising that teaching would attract males whose family experience does not compare favorably to the opportunities offered in teaching. The recruitment of males into teaching has destroyed the middle-class homogeneity typical of the profession prior to the 1950's. At least in terms of social background, the teaching profession now has less of a middle-class bias. Thus another unanticipated consequence of the recruitment of males into the profession: the division of the occupation into lower-class males and higher-class females with the net result being that the teaching profession has become more representative of the general population in terms of socio-economic characteristics.

Here we reach one of the dilemmas of social stratification theory. If people are politically as they are socially, then the role of schools in the maintenance of middle-class values should have been diminished with the influx of the lower-class males. Since schools became more socially representative of the general population, the values which they disseminated should also have become more representative. But this did not occur. In the previous chapter some explanations hinging upon the notion of the deadening effect of the teaching experience were advanced as possible explanations for the continued function of the schools as gatekeepers of middle class values even when the social composition of the teaching profession had changed.

It is probably true that the desire to reduce the socio-economic homogeneity of the teaching profession had nothing to do with the introduction of inducements to recruit males. The consequence of this inducement, however, was to make it impossible to regard teachers as horizontally mobile from middle-class backgrounds to current middle-class status, and to make it necessary to look at least at some of them as vertically mobile. Hence, if we examine the social class composition of the teaching population as a static concept, we will not learn very much. Regardless of their class origins, teachers regard themselves, and are regarded by the population, as members of the lower-middle to middle-middle class.

If teachers as members of this broadly designated segment of the population we call the middle class are typical of the behavior and values of that class, they should be expected to have moderately conservative views, lean to the Republican party, and have a preference for socially accepted behavior. These indeed are the characteristics of the teaching profession today. One might suspect, therefore, that the functional role responsibilities of system maintenance rest principally upon those teachers who are primarily mobile within the middle class rather than upon those who are vertically mobile from lower class to middle class.

Social class is probably the most pervasive independent variable in the literature of social science, but very little is known about the effects of social mobility. The reason for this probably is that, even in our relatively open society, mobility into or out of an occupation is low. Some still are more likely than not to enter their fathers' occupations, and occupationally stable people far outnumber occupationally mobile people.

The changing class composition of the teaching profession which has come about as a result of the recruitment of males provides an opportunity to study the effects of mobility upon attitudes and behavior. What are the mobility patterns of teachers? Leiberman, noting the shift in recruitment from middle to lower classes and assuming that teaching is a middle-class occupation, offers the conclusion that teachers are socially a very mobile group.[1] If this is true, then teachers are not like any other occupational group because, in the society as a whole, stability is the rule and mobility the exception. Further, Leiberman does not even consider the possibility that part of the mobility of teachers could be *downward* mobility. In part, the problem results from ambiguous usage of the concept of mobility. He does not offer any guides for the measurement of mobility, although several exist. One, therefore, still needs to know something about the extent of actual mobility in the teaching profession before talking about the effects of mobility.

Mobility, as the concept is used in this chapter, describes a teacher's situation in terms of the occupational status of his father and the current family income of the teacher. A teacher thus is situated in one of four possible groups: (1) a low-stationary group of low-income teachers whose fathers held low-status occupations; (2) a high-stationary group of high-income teachers whose fathers held high-status occupations; (3) an upward-mobile group of high-income teachers whose fathers held low-status occupations; and (4) a downward mobile group of low-income teachers whose fathers held high-status occupations.[2]

What is the distribution of each of these four possible types within the teaching profession? More than 33 per cent of the teaching population are low stationary. Only about 16 per cent of all teachers are high stationary. Thus, teachers whose current status is not better than that of their fathers form the largest single category,

---

[1] Myron Leiberman, *Education as a Profession* (Englewood Cliffs: Prentice-Hall, Inc., 1956), p. 467.

[2] The cutting point on incomes remains the same as in the previous chapter (10,000). The determination of the social class of the father is based on Hollingshead's Index of Social Position. Dividing occupations into either "high" or "low" categories from an index which originally included seven positions results in the construction of some heterogeneous categories. For purposes of ascertaining mobility, however, the problem is not too difficult. The "high" status occupations consist of those from lower-middle (such as owners of little businesses) up to upper (such as executives of large concerns). The "low" status occupations consist of those from skilled manual employees down to unskilled employees.

and they enjoy a life roughly comparable to that to which they were accustomed to as children. Very few in this category are continuing an upper-class style of life. About 33 per cent of the teachers are downward mobile, considerably in excess of the patterns established in other occupational groups; about 15 per cent are upward mobile. Thus, the upward mobile teachers are the smallest percentage of the total teaching population. It may well be that people, especially men, become teachers in the hope of economic advancement, but it is apparent that teaching provides no panacea or escape from the general pattern of stability as the rule and mobility the exception to it.

One third of the teachers who came from low-status families are upward mobile, whereas two-thirds of the teachers who came from high-status families are downward mobile. Sex differences and patterns of occupational persistence also shed some light upon the mobility of teachers. The majority of male teachers come from low-status backgrounds, the majority of female teachers come from high-status backgrounds. Projecting these proportions, one might expect most of the teachers with high-status backgrounds (i.e., those in the high-stationary and downward-mobile groups) to be females and most of the teachers with low-status backgrounds (i.e., those in the low-stationary and upward-mobile groups) to be males. However, this is not the case. It is true that there are more upward-mobile males than females, but it is also true that there are more downward-mobile males than females, while at the same time there are more high-stationary males than females. This means that the downward mobile segment of the teaching population is over-representative of males. In short, the teaching occupation contributes more than its share of downward-mobile people to society and among them there are more men teachers than would be expected.

The occupational persistence of men, even though they are downward mobile, is related to the observations of the first chapter that men, although they have no intention of doing so, actually remain in teaching longer than women. In other words, although teaching does not recruit very many men from the upper classes, those that it does recruit drift into downward mobility. Women teachers also suffer this same misfortune, but more of them get out of teaching. Most of those remaining somehow manage to maintain a stationary rather than downward-mobile position. About half the downward-mobile male teachers but only one-third of the downward-mobile female teachers have been teaching for ten or more years.

THE NATURE OF MOBILITY

The downward-mobile male high school teacher has some of the characteristics of a person trapped in a situation from which he is unable to escape. We noted that income was not especially important as an affector of the attitudes and behaviors of men teachers. This is decidedly not the case with mobility. *Social mobility* defines the process whereby individuals move from one position in society to another. People tend to rate social position as an index of prestige and since prestige is generally an important determinant of personal satisfaction, mobility can be expected to have some effect upon the outlook of those who undergo it. A person who moves up the social hierarchy seeks to exhibit the external trappings of his new position and will seek to establish contact with a new, appropriate reference group. He will seek out friends in his new rather than in his old status, and his organizational affiliations will tend to reflect his new circle of friends. The new set of reference groups provides a re-enforcement for attitudes which may have become more typical of the new class than are the attitudes of those who had always been in this class. It is said that people who are rising up the social ladder are often excessively concerned with the values of the class to which they aspire—they need to convince themselves as much as those who observe their behavior that they really belong. As Lipset and Bendix phrase it, "A person who raises his occupational status will normally seek also to raise his social status." [3] Members of the middle class who come from a working-class background are apt to be politically more conservative (at least, less likely to vote Democratic) than those of the middle class whose current status is congruent with that of their parents, much as there is no anticommunism so vigorous as that of ex-communists, no Americanism so passionate as that of immigrants. Thus the consequences of striving for status can be excessive conformity. Merton has proposed that there is a zealous

---

[3] Seymour M. Lipset and Reinhard Bendix, *Social Mobility in Industrial Society* (Berkeley and Los Angeles: University of California Press, 1960), p. 6.

and uncritical acceptance of class-related dogma, sort of anticipatory socialization, whereby people moving up the status hierarchy exhibit middle- or upper-class values and behaviors prior to their arrival in that class.[4]

West examined a group of men—call them self-made—who had worked their way through college in comparison to a group of male graduates who had earned none of their college expenses. Both of these groups had reached the top economic brackets.[5] Assuming that people in top economic brackets are Republicans, then anticipatory socialization would lead us to expect that the self-made men should be more Republican than the more privileged men. Accordingly, their economic ideologies should be more strongly *laissez-faire* than the men of traditional wealth. This did not prove to be true. The self-made men, while they were still rising up the ladder, were less likely to identify with the Republican party than were the privileged men, and they were less likely to take a strong position against government planning. However, when they had arrived, they were slightly less Republican but were more opposed to government planning than were the privileged men. It appears, therefore, that people who are rising socially may be greatly concerned with the values of the social class to which they aspire, but it takes actual presence in the class and probably some reinforcement by means of interaction with other members of it to bring this extremism to a head.

Two myths and one truth form the basis of the discussion that follows. In Chapter I it was proposed that teachers overemphasize middle-class values. This is hardly an original conclusion, and there is much evidence to show that teachers are inclined to adhere to middle-class values to the point of not giving lower-class youths fair treatment in the school program. That is the truth—the two myths are found in the most normal explanations of it.

[4] Robert K. Merton, *Social Theory and Social Structure* (New York: The Free Press of Glencoe, Inc., 1957), pp. 265-268.

[5] Patricia Salter West, "Social Mobility Among College Graduates," in Reinhard Bendix and Seymour Martin Lipset, eds., *Class, Status and Power* (New York: The Free Press), pp. 479-480. See also Seymour Martin Lipset and Reinhard Bendix, *Social Mobility in Industrial Society* (Berkeley and Los Angeles: University of California Press, 1960), pp. 66-67.

One of the clearest documentations of middle-class bias in high school teachers is Hollingshead's *Elmtown's Youth*.[6] Hollingshead demonstrated that teachers in Elmtown, a fictitious name for a small Midwestern community, consistently singled out middle- and upper-class children for preferential treatment in assigning grades and encouraging students to go to college. When upper-class children misbehaved, the teachers looked the other way; when lower-class children did the same misdeed, severe reprisals were administered. The extracurricular activities of the school were totally dominated by upper-class youths. Further, there appeared to be definite efforts to push upper-class children into the academic or college preparatory program, while lower-class students were discouraged from entering this program even if they appeared to have the intellectual ability for it.

What were the causes of this situation? Hollingshead concluded that the power structure of the community was within the control of the upper classes and that the school was an instrument of upper-class domination. Leiberman, however, who maintains that what goes on in Elmtown is typical of most school districts, draws other conclusions from Hollingshead's data. He argues, first, that teachers are socially mobile and, second, that they reflect the common tendency to overemphasize the value of the class toward which they aspire. These are the two myths of a fallacious explanation for a true situation. Teachers are not upwardly mobile and, even if they were, anticipatory socialization has certainly not been demonstrated to be a reliable predictor of the attitudes of the upwardly mobile.[7]

DOWNWARD MOBILITY AND ANXIETY

What do we know about the consequences of downward mobility? We could hardly assume a sort of reverse anticipatory socialization; that is, it would not be sensible to assume that those moving down the class ladder aspire to a lower class than that which they are in. It would seem more reasonable to expect the downwardly mobile to retain the trappings of former position, to "retain the values,

---

[6] August Hollingshead, *Elmtown's Youth* (New York: John Wiley & Sons, Inc., 1946).

[7] Myron Lieberman, *Education as a Profession* (Englewood Cliffs: Prentice-Hall, Inc., 1956), p. 468.

attitudes, norms, and standards of the class from which they are falling partly in the aspiration and hope to return."[8] Assuming that conservatism is a characteristic of the middle and upper classes, the conclusion is that both lower-class persons who were once in a high class and higher-class persons who were once in a lower class are more conservative than the traditional custodians of middle-class conservatism.

Mobility can have unsettling effects upon personality. In a society in which upward mobility is approved behavior and downward mobility is disapproved behavior, the mere act of moving, irrespective of direction, may be dysfunctional to the individual and, by so much, to the society. People are generally most comfortable in surroundings that are familiar, and a stable class position, regardless of whether it be in an upper or lower class, may contribute to individual security and lack of frustrations. Mobility, and perhaps especially downward mobility, may increase frustration and insecurity; Durkheim found suicide rates to be higher among both upward- and downward-mobile people than among stationary groups of people.[9] Hollingshead and Redlich found that lower-class people who are not upwardly mobile seem satisfied and content with their way of life. They have "a sense of personal dignity and self-esteem which sustains them. . . ."[10] These placid types contrast with the strivers who are ill satisfied with themselves and with their prestige in the community. They are not content with things as they are and are less satiable than stationary people. Upward-mobile people can hardly be thought of as a mentally disturbed group, but the incidence of insecurity and neurosis appears to be higher among the strivers than among those who are satisfied with their economic lot.

It might be reasonable to assume, therefore, that the unpleasant consequences of mobility, ranging all the way from neurosis to suicide are consequences of the fact that people who are mobile find themselves in a situation of *anomie,* a situation in which an established and easily perceivable set of norms is not available and the

[8] Bernard Berelson and Gary A. Steiner, *Human Behavior: An Inventory of Scientific Findings* (New York: Harcourt, Brace & World, Inc., 1964), p. 487.

[9] August B. Hollingshead and Frederick C. Redlich, *Social Class and Mental Illness* (New York: John Wiley & Sons, Inc., 1958), pp. 104-5.

[10] Emile Durkheim, *Suicide* (New York: The Free Press of Glencoe, 1951) pp. 246-254.

individual is thus denied a permanent set of cues. But surely this is true more of downwardly-mobile than of upwardly-mobile people. Going from rags to riches is what Americans are supposed to do, going from riches to rags is just exactly what they are supposed to not do. Granted that mobility probably contributes to confusion about norms, would not the undesirable consequences of this confusion be exaggerated when the mobility pattern is in defiance of approved patterns of behavior? It can be argued that upward-mobile people, insecure in their newly acquired status and not yet certain that they will not sink back into the class from which they rose, will be just as insecure as downward mobile people.

Most of the work done on mobility and anxiety has used prejudice as an index of insecurity and frustration. One test of the relation between status, mobility, and prejudice was made by Bettelheim and Janowitz in a study of 150 war veterans in Chicago.[11] Investigating how tensions and pressures resulting from changes in social status relate to ethnic hostility, they discovered a positive correlation between downward mobility and prejudice and between upward mobility and tolerance. An identical conclusion was reached by the authors of *The Authoritarian Personality,* but one of them later rejected this conclusion and asserted that there was no relationship between mobility and tolerance.[12] Further, a secondary analysis of the Elmira, New York voting behavior study of 1948 concluded that both upward and downward mobility contributed to prejudice.[13]

Prejudice may not be the best index of the personality integration of mobile people. A more useful analysis of the incidence of certain personality characteristics among upward- and downward-mobile people is provided by Hollingshead and Redlich. Upward-mobile

[11] Bruno Bettelheim and Morris Janowitz, *The Dynamics of Prejudice* (New York: Harper & Row, Publishers, 1950), pp. 57-61.

[12] T. W. Adorno, et al., *The Authoritarian Personality* (New York: Harper, 1950), p. 204. See also, Else Frenkel-Brunswick, "Further Explorations by a Contributor to 'The Authoritarian Personality,' " in Richard Christie and Marie Jahoda, eds., *Studies in the Scope and Method of "The Authoritarian Personality"* (New York: The Free Press of Glencoe, 1954), p. 231.

[13] Joseph Greenblum and Leonard I. Pearlin, "Vertical Mobility and Prejudice: A Socio-Psychological Analysis," in Reinhard Bendix and Seymour Martin Lipset, eds., *Class, Status, and Power* (New York: The Free Press of Glencoe, 1953), pp. 480-490.

people are apt to be uncertain about their own values and are exceedingly difficult to get along with. However, the neuroses of upward-mobile people are as nothing compared to the problems of downward-mobile people. Of these people the authors write:

> Downward-mobile persons and families are not encountered frequently in our society but when this process occurs persons subject to it are recognized by the community as troublemakers. As their behavior becomes overly antisocial they are referred with increasing frequency to psychiatrists when they do not obey the subtle rules of the game expected of them by persons in higher status positions. . . . Some of their disorders present the syndrome of a "fate" neurosis. The spell of gloom, failure, and disaster which these patients exude even when they are not depressed makes them rather unapproachable and dreaded by the therapist.[14]

SOME EFFECTS OF MOBILITY

None of the studies encountered in this review of the probable consequences of mobility take sex into account. As we have seen, male and female high school teachers have substantially different reactions to the same teaching situation. In this section we shall examine the differential behaviors of male and female mobile and stationary teachers, and their perceptions of the political and social worlds, political ideologies, and need structures. If existing theories about the consequences of social mobility are correct, we could expect mobile teachers to be considerably more restive yet politically more conservative than stationary teachers, and to have individual need structures heavily imbued with concern for status and authority.

There are not very many upward-mobile teachers, either male or female, but they are very happy with their jobs. Indeed, until they gain some experience in their jobs, the upward-mobile males are actually considerably more satisfied than the upward-mobile females. But as the upward-mobile male teacher increases his experience, he like all other males becomes progressively more dissatisfied with his job. The upward-mobile female teachers, whose early dissatisfaction is a curious deviation from the normal female pattern, soon become the category which contains the highest proportion of satisfied teach-

---

[14] Hollingshead and Redlich, *op. cit.*, p. 369.

ers. More than 80 per cent of the experienced upward-mobile female teachers are satisfied with their jobs. Most males, however, are low stationary or downward-mobile. The downward-mobile male is disapproved of by society, and he is hostage of a feminine role. It is not surprising that downward-mobile males exhibit all the symptoms of defeat and despair indigenous to the male teaching role. They hate their work.

For the upward-mobile male, recruited from the lower classes, the introduction of a measure of mobility into the educational system offers a potential for job satisfaction.

ALIENATION AND MOBILITY

Alienation is an exceedingly difficult term to define. It has its intellectual roots in Robert Merton's idea of *anomie,* a feeling of rootlessness, helplessness, and isolation manifested in a belief that one is powerless to control the events around him. Alienation is usually believed to be more dominant in the lower classes because, as Merton suggests, it is the product of the existence of socially defined goals without the provision of access to means for achieving these goals. Lower-class children are expected by society to strive to advance into the middle class. To do this, they need a good education. But as we have seen the educational establishment is biased heavily against the lower classes. The resultant frustration and alienation of many lower-class children is not a personality variable but a rational response to the structure of society.

Political alienation is the sense of being left out of the political process. People who are politically alienated believe that the basic political decisions of the community are made without concern for their values and interests, but more, that any effort on their part to participate in the political process would be futile. The lower classes have been described as particularly susceptible to political alienation.

How does mobility relate to alienation? Is a downward-mobile person as alienated as a person who is stationary within the lower class: Is an upward-mobile person as free of alienation as one who is stationary within the upper class? Or is mobility, irrespective of the direction, so unnerving as to produce a general feeling of helplessness? All three possibilities have some empirical support, as we have seen. However, in view of the fact that there is a clear relationship between the direction of mobility and the extent of satisfaction, and in view of the fact that the preponderance of evidence probably is weighed in favor of downward mobility being more unsettling than upward mobility, it seems reasonable to predict that upward-mobile people are apt to be substantially less alienated than downward-mobile people. If alienation is descriptive of a feeling of being left out of the political world, and if this feeling typically attaches to those in the lower class, then people who have entered the middle class from the lower class should experience novel feelings of enhanced power and strength. Upward-mobile teachers, then, should be considerably less alienated than low-stationary teachers and, perhaps, less alienated than high-stationary teachers.

Downward-mobile people, then, should be the most alienated, upward-mobile people the least alienated, and the stationary groups should exhibit a degree of alienation intermediate between the two extremes. Using this hypothesis as a guide, scores on an alienation scale were matched against the teachers' pattern of mobility with the result that, initially, absolutely no relationship between alienation and mobility appeared. When the upward- and downward-mobile groups were scored separately as males and females, however, the predicted pattern was correct, but only for the males. In fact the predicted pattern was exactly reversed for females. Downward-mobile males are extremely alienated but downward-mobile females are not at all alienated; upward-mobile females are extremely alienated but upward-mobile males are not. Of all female teachers upward-mobile teachers are the most alienated while among male teachers upward-mobile teachers are the least alienated. Mobility, then, produces diametrically opposite effects in the sexes.

This distribution of attitudes is especially pronounced among the teachers with more experience. One might suppose that downward-mobile males have come to realize that their status is permanent and the resulting feeling of loss of power is very great. Upward-mobile males, too, realize that their status is permanent and accordingly feel an awakening sense of great power. Why does this explanation work only for males? Why is it that factors which apparently contribute to a feeling of personal political power among males contribute to a feeling of less power among females? There are several possible explanations for the totally different impact of mobility upon alienation among males and females.

The first of these explanations requires that we recall the earlier argument that the occupation of the male is more central to his well-being, whereas for the female the income earned in teaching is more supplementary. Thus, since we are measuring current status by income, it may be true that the status of the female could undergo a more rapid shift than that of the male, depending, for example, upon what happened to her husband's salary. Since the female's status is less keyed to her teaching position, the correlation between alienation and mobility among females need not be as great. But this explanation overlooks the fact that it is not so much a matter of there being no relationship between alienation and mobility among females; rather the problem is that there is a very clear and distinct pattern which directly contradicts that of the males. This argument seems faulty, therefore, and we turn to another way of considering these phenomena.

SOME FEMININE CHARACTERISTICS OF MALE TEACHERS

It has been argued that the male, because of the masculine nature of his role and the manipulative and power-laden characteristics of politics, is more concerned with the political world than is the female. Historically, women have been assigned domestic and child-rearing roles, but not political roles. Men have taken the dominant, powerful role, assigning to women the dependent, receptive role. Consequently, as Lane observes, a woman becomes involved in politics only at the risk of reducing her feminine identity. Whether the submissive role of the woman is natural or is a cultural function is not very important.[15] What is important is that if women become active politically they may appear to have abandoned the feminine role to challenge the dominant role of the male. Duverger observed that women, "have the mentality of minors in many fields, and particularly in politics." Female acceptance of male paternalism is more typically European than American, as Almond and Verba have

[15] Robert E. Lane, *Political Life* (New York: The Free Press of Glencoe, 1959), p. 210.

shown.[16] Nevertheless, women in general do take a less active role in politics and, according to opinion samplings of the adult population of the United States, women generally are thought to be less efficacious politically than men.

Among teachers, men *are not* more efficacious than women. They are not necessarily more psychologically pleased with the political world. Considered as a political group without respect to income, mobility, or teaching experience, male and female teachers respond almost identically to questions about political alienation. Further, certain kinds of male teachers (downward mobile and high stationary) are considerably more alienated than women. Thus at the upper income level of the teaching profession men feel politically powerless. These male teachers, consequently, may be described as responding in a manner *similar to the women* reported in the national samples. Or, to re-phrase, women are responding in a "male" fashion.

It appears that men respond differently than do women to questions about political power and that, unlike the general male population, men teachers feel left out politically. I maintain that these upper-income male teachers give feminine responses to questions about political power because their playing of a feminine occupational role is brought home to them sharply by the discrepancy between their upper-class backgrounds and their current situations in a female-dominated system wherein their prestige is probably not as great as it was prior to their entry into teaching careers. The situation is especially acute for downward-mobile males.

As yet we have no firm explanation of why upward mobility should be so unsettling for upward-mobile females, an extremely alienated group. Perhaps it is that, just as males are not expected to be downward-mobile, females are not expected to be upward-mobile. Striving to make good in a career is a masculine role, and women who play this role may, as Lane suggests, fear loss of femininity. In this case, however, the loss of femininity is not a concomitant of acquisition of masculine values; rather it is an over-identification with feminine values, and alienation is the result.

[16] Maurice Duverger, *The Political Role of Women* (Paris: UNESCO, 1955), p. 129. Gabriel Almond and Sidney Verba, *The Civic Culture* (Boston: Little, Brown and Co., 1965), pp. 324-336.

MOBILITY AND CYNICISM

A person who is cynical about the worth of the political process may be alienated, his cynicism serving as a rationalization for alienation; certainly the two attitudes toward the political world are related. The relationships between mobility, alienation, and cynicism are summed up in Chart I. Like alienation, cynicism should be a

CHART I: MOBILITY AND POLITICAL PERCEPTION

Group	Alienation	Cynicism
Downward Mobile		
Males	High	High
Females	Low	Low
Upward Mobile		
Males	Low	Low
Females	High	High

product of mobility; upward-mobile people lack the cynicism apparent in downward-mobile people. However, as was true when we were talking about alienation, unless one divides the mobiles into male and female groups, there no relationship between mobility and cynicism is apparent. This is the case because the theory works only for male teachers, and not for female teachers. Regardless of the lengths of their teaching experience, downward-mobile male teachers are more cynical than other males, but upward-mobile female teachers are more cynical than other females.

MOBILITY AND TRUST IN OTHERS

Political alienation specifically denotes powerlessness to influence the making of public decisions. Suppose we consider a more general social alienation that has no direct reference to politics—the alienation felt by an individual who feels that people cannot be trusted, and that he must always be on guard to avoid being taken advantage of. For this variable, a relationship between mobility and attitudes emerges for both sexes. Upward-mobile people trust others more readily than do downward-mobile people. The pattern is especially pronounced for males, but for females the pattern is at least discernible.

The fact that the relationship between mobility and trust is sex-linked lends support to the argument that politics is particularly salient for males. However, even here it is impossible to ignore the different responses of men and women. Among both upward- and downward-mobile groups, females are more generally trusting than are males. Nearly one half of the downward-mobile females are trusting of others as compared to less than a third of the downward mobile males. Downward-mobile males, then, are the least likely to trust other people. Male teachers have been described as the underclass of the profession. Downward-mobile male teachers, it appears, are the lowest stratum of this underclass.

MOBILITY AND IDEOLOGY

If it is necessary to examine males and females separately in trying to understand the relationship between mobility and perceptions of the political world, is this also true when we examine overt political ideology?

In looking at such overt ideologies, theories guiding our inquiry are much clearer. Mobile teachers should be the most conservative, either because they are clinging desperately to the group norms of the class from which they have departed or because they are reaching frantically toward the group norms of the class toward which they are moving.

Conservative attitudes are the norm of upper-class groups, but the intensity of the conservatism of upward- and downward-mobile groups surpasses that of the high-stationary groups. Downward-mobile teachers are the most conservative of teachers, substantially more conservative than the high-stationary group of teachers. Downward-mobile teachers cling desperately to the values of the class from which they have departed.

Upward-mobile teachers are more conservative than the low-stationary group. The tendency to adopt the values of the middle class is strongest among downward-mobile people, weakest among upward-mobile people; those rising out of the lower class tend to display values that are similar neither to those of the lower class nor to those of the middle or upper classes. With regard to overt ideology (but not with regard to perceptions of power), downward mobility, and to a lesser extent upward mobility, seems to erase the reactional differences between males and females that were apparent in measures of their perceptions of the political world. This can be explained by the fact that the measures of perception of the political world provoked a feeling of alienation and a cynical response among downward-mobile males but not among downward-mobile females. Mobility has the greatest differential impact upon the sexes when matters of power and influence are at stake. Power and influence are especially acute to males, who apparently need to feel powerful and are damaged psychologically when they are deprived of that feeling. Ideological matters that do not threaten or challenge the power of the male do not elicit uniquely male responses, apparently.

MOBILITY, THE TEACHING EXPERIENCE, AND NEED FOR RESPECT

Males have a deep need to be respected, irrespective of income level or teaching experience. Does mobility exert an effect on the needs of the male for respect? It seems reasonable to suppose that there is a relationship between a feeling of powerlessness and the need for respect, that people who feel politically or socially impotent would have a craving for the respect of others. This prediction is correct; approximately 46 per cent of the people who are alienated have a high need for respect, compared to only 24 per cent of those who are not alienated. These relationships are true for both sexes.

Problems of power and respect are most acute for male teachers who come from high-status families. As children and perhaps as young adults, their position in society accustomed them to a respect they cannot derive from the teaching experience. This tension does not seem to affect either women or men having low-status backgrounds, and upward-mobile men are especially immune to this particular problem. For them, getting ahead in the world is a partial compensation for doing woman's work; for the downward-mobile men there are no ameliorating factors. The need of male teachers from low-status backgrounds for respect actually diminishes with experience—the longer they teach, the less their need (see Table I). Just the opposite is true of male teachers from high-status backgrounds—the longer they teach, the greater their need. Downward-mobile and high-stationary males who began their teaching careers without exceptional need for respect soon became almost obsessed

TABLE I: PERCENTAGE OF TEACHERS HAVING
A HIGH NEED FOR RESPECT

Group	Short Experience	Long Experience	Change
Low Stationary			
Males	35	28	− 7
Females	24	29	+ 5
Upward Mobile			
Males	33	23	−10
Females	18	19	+ 1
Downward Mobile			
Males	37	42	+ 5
Females	35	27	− 8
High Stationary			
Males	26	40	+14
Females	24	12	−12

with the problem of maintaining authority and classroom discipline. For these teachers income is unrelated to need for respect. For them, the memory of the past seems to loom large; whether or not they are presently well off economically, they crave respect. The very high need for respect, radical conservatism, extreme alienation, and cynicism of these teachers can be interpreted as reactions to their unfortunate positions in the environment which surrounds them.

RECAPITULATION

We have established that income and length of teaching experience are not as important as sex in determining teacher behavior. In this chapter we subjected this view to a further test by introducing the factor of mobility. It was found that some of the consequences of teachers' social mobility can be understood only in terms of sex; this is especially true of matters affecting the political or personal power of the male.

Changing social status entails an element of uncertainty and normlessness. For both males and females, the uncertainties of mobility translate into alienation and cynicism, but the pattern is one of opposites: downward-mobile males and upward-mobile females are the alienated, cynical ones. The majority of male teachers come from low-status backgrounds, the majority of females from high-status backgrounds, but because of their greater teaching longevities, males are disproportionately represented among the downward-mobile teachers. The political values of mobile teachers fluctuate far more through time than do the political values of stationary teachers. The least fluctuation occurs among high-stationary teachers; the greatest, among upward-mobile teachers. Downward-mobile teachers are conservative by any index of conservatism, but upward-mobile teachers are not typified by conservatism, even after they have arrived in the upper classes. This means that the teaching profession harbors a significant number of people whose attitudes toward society are in flux if they are not firmly hostile and negative.

The implications of this for our political and educational systems should not be minimized. Almond and Verba noted that in Great Britain and the United States more citizens feel they can influence government decisions than is true of citizens in Germany, Italy, or Mexico. They believe that the American and British respondents' perceptions of personal power are related to the stable democratic political systems of these two nations. They do not maintain that all citizens who feel that they could influence government have actually done so, but they do believe that the attitudes of a democratic citizenry should include the belief that one can participate meaningfully in politics if and when he wants to. If an individual believes he possesses a reservoir of political power, he is more likely to be an active participant in the political process, but if he sees himself as left out of the political process, he is not likely to make the effort to become a politically active citizen. The latter is the spirit prevailing among downward-mobile teachers—they vote less frequently than other teachers, and they are not so active in professional organizations. Their behavior is symptomatic of their feelings of powerlessness.

Litt makes the point that it is a major socialization function of the schools to instill within the student a high sense of citizen duty. But textbooks do not teach themselves, they have to be interpreted to the students by a teacher. Is it possible for teachers who are cynical and alienated about the political process to convey to their students how necessary it is to participate in the political process? If a teacher believes that participation in the process is futile, can he conceal his sense of futility and frustration from students and successfully teach them how to become politically responsible citizens? In Chapter I it was hypothesized that our schools do not provide students with an alternative to acceptance of the *status quo*. It is possible, however, that downward-mobile male teachers and upward-mobile female teachers offer students at least a hint that ours is perhaps not the best of all possible worlds. Thus, teacher-recruitment patterns may have brought into the educational system an unanticipated alternative to the cheery optimism and bland conformism of high school textbooks.

Part Two

The task now is to describe the behavior of these teachers within the institutional setting of the educational system and to decide whether or not their reactions to the teaching experience, their recruitment, and their attitudes toward their work translate into overt patterns of behavior. In the first section, attention was concentrated upon the relationship between environmental conditions (such as mobility, income, sex, and length of time teaching) and attitudes. The main theoretical thrust rested upon role theory. Because men and women teachers react to the expectations imposed upon the status of teachers in different ways, their political attitudes and perceptions are quite different. Just as there is a link between roles and attitudes, there is a link between roles, attitudes, and—as will be discussed in this section—behavior. Eulau makes this point quite clearly: "We speak of the father's role, the teacher's role, the minister's role, the judge's role, and so on. What we mean in all of these instances is that a person is identified by his role and that, in interpersonal relations activating the role, he behaves, will behave, or should behave in certain ways." [1] In this book, we have bisected the teachers role into the male and female teacher's role. Up to this point, the use of the theory of roles has helped in the understanding of attitudes, but does it, as Eulau suggests, help in understanding behavior when the role is activated? What sort of situations activate the role of teachers? Three, which are discussed in the next chapters, come readily to mind. Obviously the teacher role is activated by the professional organization which represents, or is supposed to represent, the teacher politically and professionally. Also, the classroom situation activates the teacher role, perhaps to the exclusion of other competing roles. Finally, the teacher's role is activated when

[1] Heinz Eulau, *The Behavioral Persuasion in Politics* (New York: Random House, 1963) pp. 39-40.

the community applies—or is believed to apply—sanctions against activity or expression on the part of teachers. Can the separate analysis of male and female teachers help us in understanding their behavior in professional organizations? It should, because activity in such organizations is especially linked to the teacher's day-to-day life within the educational system. Therefore, what do male teachers, generally dissatisfied with their jobs, think of educational associations which are supposed to improve their lot? Do they work actively within the educational associations to remedy the evils of the educational system? Or does their generally discouraged attitude prevent them from participating in united activities? What about behavior in the classroom? Do the perceptions of male teachers stimulate them to become expressive, irrespective of the consequences? Or does their distrust of the educational establishment influence them to "play it safe?" Finally, we need to know about different reactions to sanctions imposed upon teachers from within the educational system and from the broader community. Where do most of the sanctions originate and what kinds of teachers are likely to modify their behavior because of potential sanctions?

Chapter Three:
THE
TEACHERS ASSOCIATION:
DOES IT
REPRESENT TEACHERS?

Most teachers belong to teachers associations, which, like other formal organizations, perform functions both for society as a whole and for the individuals who belong to them. For society, the existence of a large number of formal organizations appears to correlate with a high degree of citizen involvement in community affairs. Political stability is encouraged by the maintenance of a large and well-organized system of formal organizations. For the individual, the formal organization can mediate him and the environment by functioning as a transmitter of information, and can represent his claims in a manner more influential than would be possible for him operating as an individual.

An interest group successfully mediates on behalf of an individual when it provides him with the influence of an organization through which to voice and subsequently gain satisfaction for his demands. A formal organization can satisfy the maintenance needs of the political system only when it satisfies the demands of its members. Interest-group members must be sufficiently satisfied with the organization to be willing to accord it the function of mediator in order for the group to perform its societal function.

Does the educational association satisfy the demands of its members? In this chapter some possible answers to this question will be suggested. The emphasis of the discussion will be on (1) Proper organizational goals, (2) modes of participation, (3) extent and distribution of member satisfaction, and (4) the organization's influence upon the values and behavior of the members. The ability of educational organizations to satisfy the needs of teachers may be a crucial determinant of the course of future educational policy.

Most state education associations are old, well established, and according to legislators, influential in the lobbying process; most teachers belong to one or more of them. But competition from teachers' unions for the loyalties of teachers is increasing. In 1961 New York City's teachers voted to be represented by the United Federation of Teachers, the New York City affiliate of the American Federation of Teachers. The union received more than twice as many votes as the National Education Association affiliate. In several states teachers have walked off the job to dramatize demands for higher wages. In many of the nation's larger cities unions are waging a consistent struggle against National Education Association state affiliates for the right to represent teachers. In Portland, Oregon, for example, the established Oregon Education Association is being threatened by the less potent but faster-growing Portland Federation of Teachers, an AFL-CIO affiliate. The union submitted a slate of opposition candidates to the teachers in an election to choose a committee to consult with school boards on teachers' salaries. The NEA was sufficiently alarmed about the union threat that it sent personnel to help direct the campaign in Portland. The Oregon Education Association won the election, but it did not necessarily stem the growing revolution of urban teachers. A year prior to the election the Portland Classroom Teachers Association withdrew from the Oregon Education Association and subsequently gave its support to the Portland Federation of Teachers. Further, the union received full support from teachers' associations in the metropolitan area that were still affiliated with the Oregon Education Association and the NEA.

The revolt of the Portland teachers typifies the growing militancy of teachers throughout the nation. More than 100 teacher strikes have occurred in the last twenty-five years. The struggle really centers around the professional image of the teacher, with the NEA affiliates and the labor unions offering different teacher images. The revolt against the teachers associations is primarily an urban phenomenon, led by males. The significance of this will become apparent as we examine the distribution of satisfactions among teachers.

WHY TEACHERS JOIN ASSOCIATIONS

Lieberman wrote that "the foremost fact about teachers organizations in the United States is their irrelevance in the national scene." [1] To what extent do teachers agree with this indictment? To begin to answer this question we need to know why teachers join teachers associations. Basically, there are three motivations for joining. First, teachers join because they think it will help them professionally and intellectually. Second, they join variously because they believe they are expected to, or they are requested to, or in some cases they are pressured to join by school administrators. Third, they join because they believe that they can increase their individual political power by casting their lot with an organization that can lobby for them and, if necessary, defend them against community attacks.

Most teachers join out of the first motivation. They want to expose themselves to professional literature and ideas, which they believe will lead to the improvement of their teaching and thereby raise the standards of the profession generally. However, about one fourth of the teachers who join do so because they are coerced into doing so. Teachers unions have claimed that NEA membership would be cut by half if administrative pressure on teachers was ceased. This seems an exaggerated estimate, but administrative pressure *is* greater than the NEA itself concedes. In some states, school superintendents authorize salary deductions for NEA membership to be made without prior consultation with the affected teachers. In other states, the situation is not so overt, but teachers nonetheless get the message that the smart thing to do is join up. Those teachers are probably aware of the fact that in the evaluation forms used in deciding promotions and tenure membership in professional organizations is a criterion. Especially in rural and small-town school districts the drive for a 100 per cent NEA membership often gets the official blessing of school administrators and lay people on school boards alike.

The NEA estimates that about 13 per cent of its members join

[1] Myron Lieberman, *The Future of Public Education* (Chicago: University of Chicago Press, 1960), 179.

in response to administrative pressure. This appears to be an under-estimate, but even so the NEA data point up some interesting things. Administrative pressure is felt more at the secondary than at the elementary level, and more by male than by female teachers. Too, administrative pressure is much more of a motivation to teach-ers who have been teaching less than three years than it is to more experienced teachers—the greater the teaching experience, the greater the resistance to administrative pressure. This suggests that either the younger teachers are more sensitive or that they are more correct. Teachers in small school districts felt administrative pres-sure much more severely than teachers in urban or metropolitan districts. Thus NEA membership is made compulsory or at least semi-compulsory in the very areas where antilabor sentiment is the most vigorous.

The voluntary nature of membership in teachers associations is clearly being compromised, and a modified union shop exists. In-deed, teachers associations appear to be somewhat similar to the unions. Compulsory union membership is a legal requirement for getting a job in a union shop. In the case of teachers, compulsory teachers association membership is a subtle, often concealed, but nonetheless real condition of keeping a job. Leaders of education associations are certain to object to this likening of teachers associ-ations to labor unions, but the similarities are real.

The antipathy of the NEA toward teachers unions is delightfully illustrated by a 1957 NEA research bulletin reporting the response to a questionnaire on the extent of organizational affiliations among teachers.[2] Appended to the text of the report are the questions used. Since it was a mail questionnaire, closed alternative questions were used, and the organizations which the teachers could choose from were limited to the NEA and its affiliates. We find, however, the following addendum to the closed alternative questions. "Local teachers union (write-in response, not in answer checklist)."! Assum-ing that the 2 per cent of the teachers who made the write-in re-sponse accurately reflected union membership in 1957, the unions had recruited approximately 47,000 teachers. In the ten years fol-lowing, union membership doubled. Significantly, the response to

[2] National Education Association, *The American Public School Teacher,* 1960-61 (NEA: April, 1963).

the NEA questionnaire revealed that union membership was greatest among male urban secondary school teachers.

A small minority of teachers join associations because of political motivations. Typical of such motivations are the beliefs that the association can present a good case for teachers in the legislature, and that salary increases can be expected to result from the lobbying efforts of state teachers organizations, most of which do engage in vigorous lobbying programs and employ experienced, skilled lobbyists.

The paucity of political motives for joining an organization is not surprising, and it does not necessarily inhibit the political activities of the organization. Most people do not concern themselves as much with politics as with other day-to-day problems of existing. Hence, when they join an organization that performs a multitude of functions, it is to be expected that political reasons for joining will rank rather low except, of course, if it is a political club or other overly political organization. In this respect, a teachers organization is again somewhat similar to a union: unions are persistent actors in the political process, but they also perform other services for their members, and many union members do not concern themselves with the political activities of their organization. This human failing, however, does not inhibit the political activities of unions any more than of teachers associations.

The motivations which a person has for remaining in an organization may undergo substantial change according as he becomes active or remains passive in it. People who join an organization for primarily nonpolitical reasons may become highly motivated politically by the activities of the organization, if they are convinced that this activity is likely to strengthen professional communication.

Teachers associations are somewhat inhibited in their political activity because of the belief among teachers that, as members of a profession (a status teachers cultivate), their professional organizations should be above politics. The fear is that the stature of the teacher as a professional will suffer if the organization gets involved in the rough-and-tumble of politics, especially electoral politics. There is a division of opinion as to what role teachers organizations should play in electoral politics. This division appears to be a stable one. The few teachers who join a teachers organization for political reasons are far more likely to want the organization to take an active role in the electoral process than are those who joined for nonpolitical reasons.

Excluding the highly politically motivated minority, most teachers envision only a modest political role for their organizations. Considered as a whole, teachers are far more willing to support so-called defense activities than they are willing to support political activities. They agree that the organization should exert its energies to defend teachers under attack from the community, but they think it unbecoming the organization to sponsor politicians sympathetic to the goals of public education. *Politics and education do not mix* is a slogan that seems to guide the thinking of many teachers. Teachers have no objections to the lobbying functions of their organizations, however. The lobbying programs of state teachers organizations are much more thoroughly developed than are their electoral programs. The administrative staffs of state organizations are more openly inclined to favor the involvement of teachers in electoral process than the teachers are, yet the administrative staff believes teachers to be much more reluctant to get involved than the teachers actually are. Teachers associations occasionally endorse political candidates and take sides on public issues, but they do so much less often than labor unions do. Legislative politics absorbs most of their political energies. Headquarters staffs include government relations specialists responsible for lobbying, and members receive periodic reports about the progress of lobbying programs. They regard lobbying as one of the services they pay dues for.

WHAT KIND OF TEACHERS ARE ACTIVE
IN EDUCATIONAL ASSOCIATIONS?

Like all organizations, educational associations are embodiments of Bryce's classic description of formal organizations:

> In all assemblies and groups and organized bodies of men, from a nation down to the committee of a club, direction and decision rest in the hands of a small percentage, less and less in proportion to the larger and larger size of the body, until in a great population

it becomes an infinitesimally small proportion of the whole number. This is and always has been true of all forms of government, though in different degrees.[3]

Michels succinctly observed that "who says organization, says oligarchy." [4] It is hardly a novel situation, then, that the rank and file membership of teachers associations is passive.

In 1963, the NEA maintained that 54 per cent of the members of teachers organizations were active members. How true such estimates are probably depends on how one defines an active member. It may well be true that a majority of teachers are active in the sense that they pay their dues regularly and read the professional literature of the organization. A more realistic appraisal of active membership was provided by the NEA in 1957 when it estimated that about 15 per cent gave as the NEA put it, much time and effort to the work of the association. The apathy of the average member is understandable. Teachers, like members of other organizations, prefer to spend most of their nonworking time either with their families, their friends, or engaging in some form of recreation, relaxation, or entertainment. Most teachers, after winding up a hard day in the classroom, are simply not going to spend their spare time working at activities encouraged by the professional association. What sort of people, then, make up the active minority? To what extent are the attitudes of this active minority representative of the larger passive majority's attitudes? What sort of members of teachers organizations derive personal satisfaction from intense activity in those organizations? What effect does such intense participation have upon the attitudes and behavior of the teacher-participants?

Men, generally dissatisfied with the teaching profession, might be expected to have little desire to participate in the organizations that symbolize teaching, yet for the same reason unhappy with their situation they might envision and accordingly use the educational association as an instrument to improve their status. The NEA claims

[3] James Bryce, *Modern Democracies* (New York: The MacMillan Company, 1921), II, 542.
[4] Robert Michels, *Political Parties* (New York: The Free Press of Glencoe, Inc., 1949. p. 401.

that men are more active in educational organizations than women are. However, I dispute this claim and maintain that the active minority in teachers associations consists mostly of female teachers.

For both males and females, participation in teachers organizations increases with experience in the association but the increase is more pronounced for women. For both men and women members who have not been in an organization very long, participation is extremely low, and the difference between the sexes of participation intensity is slight. Both men and women start out with about the same intensity of participation, but for women the attraction of the organization is considerably greater and it gradually induces them to intensify their participation. This is to say that teachers associations attract participation from those teachers who have the fewest complaints about the educational establishment. Teachers in high-income groups participate more than those in low-income groups; those in downward-mobile groups participate least of all. But whether they are mobile or stationary, of high income or low, females participate more than males. Downward-mobile males are the most passive group of teachers, and it is significant that they are most dissatisfied with the educational establishment. Because teachers associations do not elicit enthusiasm from the disadvantaged segments of the teaching population, they probably reflect the conservative and views of satisfied, comfortable teachers. This helps us to understand why males dominate the union movement: males do not believe they can achieve their goals through teachers associations, since they look elsewhere. A more explicit list of their grievances will be discussed later. At any rate, the typical member of the active minority in a teachers association is a high-income female teacher with a relatively long history of participation in the association.

As was the case when we considered job satisfaction differentials, the question emerges as to whether the differentials arise as a function of the teaching profession or as a function of being male or female. If it is generally true that in most organizations females are more active than males, then the educational association is a normal organization whose female members are behaving typically. The evidence on this point is unclear. Milgrath concludes that men are more likely than women to be active in groups.[5] Almond and Verba[6] found that in the United States the female members of organizations are more likely to participate in them actively than are male members. The only criterion of activeness used by Almond and Verba was whether or not a person had held an office in an organization, but Scott,[7] using criteria other than office-holding, also found women to be more active.

In the general population, it appears, females are less likely than males to join organizations. Almond and Verba found that in the United States 68 per cent of the males but only 47 per cent of the females belong to at least one organization. For teachers, however, this relationship is reversed. Not only are more females more active in educational associations, more of them belong to organizations in addition to educational associations. About two-thirds of the male teachers who belong to an educational association belong to at least one organization, which roughly reflects the national male behavior pattern established by the Almond-Verba study. Yet, 75 per cent of the female teachers in the United States belong to at least one organization. Plainly they are more organization-prone than are male teachers, and considerably more so than nonteaching females. Moreover, female teachers are more likely to have multiple memberships than are male teachers. This seems to be evidence of the influence of occupational role-playing upon behavior. In this behavior, however, female teachers appear to be more masculine than females in the general population. The conclusion that male teachers are in this behavior more feminine than males in the general population does not seem to apply here, since there is no appreciable difference between the two groups.

Women move in and out of the teaching profession, hence it might be expected that their participation would be less than that of men who remain in the teaching profession. Feminization and the concomitant pattern of intermittent employment have fre-

---

[5] Lester Milbrath, *Political Participation* (Chicago: Rand McNally & Co., 1965), 135.

[6] Gabriel Almond and Sidney Verba, *The Civic Culture* (Boston: Little, Brown and Co., 1965), p. 259.

[7] John C. Scott, "Membership and Participation in Voluntary Associations," *American Sociological Review*, 22 (June, 1957), pp. 351-376.

quently been suggested as explanations for the difficulty of building an effective professional organization. Lieberman states:

> The woman teacher interested chiefly in marriage and a home is not likely to take a strong interest in raising professional standards and in improving the conditions of teaching. Indeed, such women are frequently opposed to raising professional standards; such action runs contrary to *their* personal long-term interest. The difficulty of building a strong professional teachers organization should be manifest. The turnover in membership is apt to be so high that teachers organizations must expend a considerable portion of their resources just to maintain a stable membership.[8]

Caplow, observing that well-organized occupations have been able to prevent the entry of women, concludes that discontinuity of employment is fatal to the development of organizational solidarity.[9] Yet the fact of the matter is that despite the tendency of women to drift in and out of the teaching profession they strengthen rather than weaken the functions of the professional organization. Since the theory does not explain the facts, a different explanation is needed.

There is a positive relationship between job satisfaction and organizational participation: the greater one's job satisfaction, the more intense his participation. Despite the intermittent nature of their careers, the greater job satisfaction experienced by and the professional commitment of women teachers encourages them to be active in all organizations concerned with the problems of the day by day performance of an occupational role.

A final and somewhat ironic comment about the active minority: small-town teachers, especially those who were raised in small towns, are more active than city teachers, and professional associations find their strongest support in nonurban areas, which contain a minority of the teachers. Administrative pressure to join teachers organizations is greatest in these areas and hence may be a partial cause of the greater activity of small-town teachers. Also, in some states, tenure is given to teachers only in the larger cities, making the pres-

[8] Myron Lieberman, *Education as a Profession*. (Englewood Cliffs: Prentice-Hall, Inc., 1956), p. 253.
[9] Theodore Caplow, *The Sociology of Work* (Minneapolis: University Minnesota Press, 1954), p. 246.

sure to join even more impressive since the threat of unemployment is present. The irony of the situation occurs in the fact that active members of educational associations are likely to be small-town female teachers who were raised in a small town and whose family income is high. The active minority, then, is not representative of the ecological makeup of the passive majority. Even greater significance attaches to the fact that the female-dominated active minority and the male-dominated passive majority have substantially different ideologies about both education and politics. It is understandable why male teachers do not believe they can improve their status by working through a teachers organization.

WHAT THE ORGANIZATION SHOULD DO: MALE AND FEMALE PERCEPTIONS

This brings us to one of the basic points of conflict between male and female teachers: the proper role of the educational organization in politics. If men have an image of themselves as individuals participating intensely in the political process, is it true that their image of the educational association is more political than is the image of women? If so, then the relatively inactive electoral role of the organization could be a source of conflict between men and women. Even though women take a more active organizational role, this organizational role is not necessarily equivalent to a political role. In other words, activity in the organization need not be related to their perception of the correct role of the organization.

Male teachers definitely regard the educational association as more of a political organization than female teachers do. Both men and women support the lobbying role of the organization but they have deeply divergent perceptions of the proper roles of the organization in educational politics and in general politics. For men, little distinction between the various kinds of elections is made. Roughly the same proportion, 50 per cent, want the organization to support candidates in school board elections, state legislative elections, or any other kind of elections. Women, however, make a great distinction between the relative proprieties of organizational involvements in school and general elections. As women teachers acquire more experience within an organization, their belief that the organization should involve itself in school elections deepens sharply. Among those women teachers who have considerable organizational experience, a majority support involvement of the organization in school elections but only about one fourth of them believe that the organization should involve itself in general elections. The greater their organizational experience the less likely are female teachers to support involvement of the organization in general elections. Experience within an organization decreases the desire of women to see its political role expanded but increases their desire to see it become vigorously involved in school board elections.

Relatively little shift in their perception of the proper role of the organization occurs as the organizational experience of men increases. Among organizationally inexperienced teachers of both sexes, males are in general the more politically vigorous. As their organizational experience increases, the vigor of males remains constant with regard to school elections while the enthusiasm of the females increases; with regard to general elections, the enthusiasm of males remains relatively constant, while the enthusiasm of females dwindles.

Women are more deeply involved in educational organizations, hence it is not surprising that their attitudes toward organizational roles vary more than do those of men. On the other hand, because women are so enthusiastic to involve the organization in school politics, one might expect that women would take a very active part in school election politics. It does not work out that way, however. Typically, men are a slightly higher proportion of those who involve themselves in local school problems, such as bond issue referendums. It appears, then, that the female teacher looks upon educational politics as a legitimate function of the educational organization, but men wish the organization would extricate itself from purely educational matters and make itself felt as a pervasive political force in the world.

If educational associations, which have recently been debating whether or not they should follow the example of the unions and endorse political candidates were to significantly expand all their varied activities they might lose support from women but would probably enjoy an increasing support among men. The majority of high school teachers are male, but high school teachers are in the minority to elementary school teachers, practically all of whom are women. Educational associations try to speak for the entire profession, so their conservatism may be wise, in terms of the calculus of support. The growing attraction of teachers unions to men becomes understandable when we notice their frustration with the relatively tame behavior of the teachers associations. As long as they adhere to the feminine preference for a restricted political role, teachers associations will be unable to serve as a channel of communication between the male teacher and the political environment. The teachers association is performing its mediating role for women, not for men.

THE ORGANIZATION AS A STIMULATOR OF POLITICAL ACTIVITY

According to students of democratic consensus a multiplicity of voluntary organizations is functional for a democracy because they encourage citizens to take active part in the affairs of the democracy. In Lane's words, "Isolation tends to make a person politically apathetic. Group memberships in themselves increase political interest and activity." [10]

The teachers association offers this assumption an acute test. Female members take a more active organizational role but a less active political role than male members. Men are less likely to participate actively in the teachers association, but those that do are also likely to participate actively in the general political process. Organizational participation does not stimulate women to great political activity. Active women are not much more likely than passive women to vote in elections, to take part in political party activities, to support candidates financially, to wear campaign buttons, and so forth. The view that specific organizational activity stimulates general political activity, therefore, seems less applicable to women than to men, whose predisposition to engage in political activity is greater to begin with. It really can not be argued that participation in an organization *causes* general political participation. It may well be that male teachers who take an active part in teachers associations find in those associations just one of numerous outlets for intense personal energies.

[10] Robert E. Lane, *Political Life* (New York: The Free Press of Glencoe, Inc., 1965), p. 187.

Men in general regard themselves as serving a more legitimate political function than women serve, and among male teachers the organizationally active ones are substantially more inclined to see themselves as fulfilling a legitimate and valuable political role than are passive members. Whether women are active or passive in the organization does not seem to affect their attitudes toward their personal political lives. A slight majority of both active and passive female teachers believe that politics is a legitimate feminine function and that they are entitled to express their political values. Most male teachers are passive organization members and define their personal political roles accordingly; that is, as roughly comparable to the role defined by female teachers.

There is a curious ambivalence about male teachers: they want to be involved in a political organization, but except for a few, they do not exert themselves to make a personal contribution to an increasing political role for their teachers association. Their organizational perceptions are typically masculine, their personal perceptions are typically feminine. As members of the active minority, male teachers differ from female teachers on the basis of the broader male political participation and the male belief that males should personally engage actively in politics.

What is true of political participation and role perception is especially true of a particular kind of role perception which I refer to as *belief in political participation with a risk of sanctions*. Teachers like clergymen are subjects of continuous, close public scrutiny. Certain behaviors that are perfectly acceptable for other occupations are (at least according to teachers) very risky for those whose job involves the training of youth. For example, there is a great deal of difference between joining a political party or serving as a precinct worker and joining, say, a civil rights organization and taking part in public demonstrations. The former sort of activity is well established and traditional within the political system; teachers are supposed to instill within their students just such a desire to participate in political activities. However, taking an active part in civil rights activities is an entirely different matter. It does not have the legitimacy of tradition, and it is radical in the sense that those who engage in public demonstrations are representing a demand for quick change of the *status quo*.

Most teachers view participation in the first type of activity as harmless; in the second, as potentially very dangerous to their professional careers. Teachers differentiate activities as those which they believe would be likely to elicit sanctions by the community or the school administration and those which they believe would be condoned or encouraged by those empowered to impose sanctions. There is an essential difference between a teacher's belief that one should participate in politics when such participation involves nothing more than wearing buttons, going to meetings, and working for candidates, and the belief that one should participate in politics even if to do so involves a form of participation more extreme than the community can be depended upon indubitably to tolerate.

It is hardly surprising that relatively few teachers believe they should engage in behaviors that invite sanction. Almost 60 per cent of all teachers believe that it is proper and desirable to take part in what can be called safe political activity, but only 20 per cent believe that it is desirable and proper to take part in sanctionable activities.

Of the majority of those teachers who are active participants in the organization there is practically no difference in the relative willingnesses of males and females to take risks. Among the most intense participants, however, about twice as many men as women indicate a willingness to engage in risky political activity. Indeed, females who are inactive members of the organization are more inclined to take political activity risks than those who are active; the reverse is true for men. Thus, activity within the organization produces exactly opposite effects in the sexes. Participation enhances the risk-taking inclinations of men but inhibits the risk-taking inclinations of women. It is clear that participation in an organization does not necessarily contribute to a feeling that one should express oneself, even though the consequences of this expression might be severe. It is appropriate to describe the organizationally active male as highly expressive and the organizationally active female as very quiescent, whether their behaviors involve safe political activity, risky political activity, or even the expressions of opinion within the classroom.

If teachers could feel certain that the collective strength of their educational association would rise to defend their behavior, if need be, they might be the more willing to engage in risky political activities. Inadvertently, in such circumstances, teachers associations might be put in the position of nurturing radical political manifestations. As we shall see, male teachers, at least, do not trust the organization to defend them if they become embroiled in a community controversy, and therefore their organizational activity probably has nothing to do with their risk-taking proclivities. It cannot be said that their active participation in an organization contributes to a feeling of personal security and, therefore, to their willingness to take risks, nor does it appear that active males find something in the organization that active females do not and, as a consequence, behave differently than females. The more likely probability is that the expressive nature of the active male is a product of a general personality structure—*because* he is expressive he takes an active role in the organization.

THE EXTENT OF MEMBER SATISFACTION

Describing organization equilibrium, Simon argues that individuals are induced to participate in an organization when their activity contributes to their personal well-being.[11] Participation is, then, a payment by the individual to the organization in return for services the organization can offer him in return. We have found females to be more active participants than males, hence we assume that the inducements to participate in educational organizations are greater for them than for males. It follows too that women are more satisfied with such organizations than men are. If this is true, the socializing effect of such organizations upon the active males must be rather minimal.

Up to this point we have described participation in an organization only in terms of the more formal aspects of voting in organizational elections, attendance at meetings, and the like. There is a kind of informal participation that may be of greater importance, however: personal contact between the leaders and the led. Among the rank and file membership, not only do women take a more active role in formal organizational business, they also have a

[11] Herbert Simon, *Administrative Behavior* (New York: The MacMillan Co., 1957), pp. 16-18, 110-112.

greater frequency of informal contact with the elected and the administrative leaders of the organization. However, among the active minority, men have considerably more personal contact with leaders. Males are frequently initiators of communication with the leadership whereas females are passive receivers of communications from above.

That males initiate communication and females receive communication gives us a clue to relative male-female satisfaction with educational associations. Male teachers initiate communication when they have something to gripe about, so there is a relationship between the initiation of contact with the leadership and general dissatisfaction with the organizational performance. Both the initiation of communication and general dissatisfaction are characteristic of men. Women find educational organizations extremely compatible with their views and therefore are content to receive rather than initiate communication.

Of course, we would expect that the tendency to agree with the goals of an organization increase with the activity of an individual within that organization. If an individual is active it is at least partially because his personal values and the values of the organization are compatible. In ascertaining the extent to which teachers believe that there is no substantial conflict between their personal goals and the goals of the organization it was found that among both males and females activity and perceived compatibility are positively correlated. The important aspect of this finding is that, whereas 75 per cent of the active males find themselves in substantial agreement with the organization, an almost unbelievable 97 per cent of the women do so. Hence, even the active men find more to disagree with than do women. Among women, organizational goals and personal goals are practically identical.

Agreement with over-all policy is important and probably colors other kinds of responses but there are other indices of satisfaction with an organization. One is the opinions members have about their individual efficacies within the over-all power structure of the organization. A member's *perception* of his influence is not a reliable index of his actual influence, but perceptions of influence do give us an expression of the attitudinal basis for organizational participation. Those who believe they wield great influence are probably likely to take a more active role than those who feel that their influence is very circumscribed. Almond and Verba, in a study of the feelings of subjective confidence entertained by respondents in five nations, concluded that the belief that one is influential is probably antecedent to efforts to wield influence.[12] It is not surprising to learn, therefore, that women, who are the most active participants in teachers associations, believe that they have great personal power within the organization.

A vital source of this power is the trust that they place in the elected leadership of the associations. Among both men and women trust of leadership increases considerably with longevity of organizational experience, but women are steadfastly more trusting than men. Women are inclined to believe that the leadership of the organization would "understand" their personal problems. Men, on the other hand, are more likely to believe that the leadership might listen politely but wouldn't care very much.

Interestingly enough, the belief women hold that the leadership is on their side translates into an objective evaluation of the actual performance of the organization. Consider, for example, members' estimation of the ability of the organization to lobby successfully for across-the-board salary increases. This is an organizational activity universally approved of by the membership. On the question of how successful members believe their education association's lobbying to be, only about one third of the male teachers but a majority of the female teachers imputed great influence to the organization.

Intimately involved in the success and the failures of the organization, the administrative staff regards its role as more significant than the rank-and-file do. The staff correctly perceives that there is often substantial dissatisfaction with its past performance, but the leaders often perceive substantially more dissatisfaction in the ranks than actually exists there. In short, they do not feel appreciated, a general characteristic, perhaps, of political leaders. In a study of community leaders charged with the responsibility of advising the board of education of a large city about the most desirable way of building a new high school, it was found that these leaders con-

---

[12] Gabriel Almond and Sidney Verba, *The Civic Culture* (Boston: Little, Brown and Co., 1965), pp. 188-204.

sistently overestimated community dissatisfaction with the plans for the school.

Another way of plumbing the membership's sentiment on organizational performance is to invite opinions, not about its actual political power, but about the sincerity of the organization's efforts to achieve results through the political process. It may be that men think the organization has little political power but that it is trying as hard as it can. About one-third of the men impute political power to the organization but nearly one-half of them think that it is doing the best it can with regard to continued efforts toward salary improvement. As to the women, they are much more satisfied —more than two-thirds of them have these attitudes. The fact that female teachers both trust the organization and believe that it is doing a good job presents an interesting correlation between a subjective evaluation of an organization and the perceived behavior of the organization. The credibility one is willing to impute to an agent is a gauge of how well the agent is believed to be performing its job. For example, teachers believe that educational associations should defend them should the community attack classroom teaching of controversial social or political issues. Are such attacks frequent? The answer varies accordingly as men or women are doing the opining. About a majority of the active men indicated that they had heard of such attacks as compared with only about one third of the women. Apparently men are more attuned than women to the problems of teaching high school in a potentially hostile environment. But they see themselves as relatively helpless against such attacks, for all that they could depend on the organization. Forty-one per cent of the active male teachers but only 14 per cent of the females said that when the attack took place the educational association either did nothing or actually went along with the attack. Only 6 per cent of the males were of the opinion that the educational association had defended the teacher under attack, but 17 per cent of the females held this opinion. Men are not only more bound up in conflict situations than women are, they are substantially more cynical about the ability or willingness of an educational organization to come to their defense.

The faith of women in the leadership of the organization can be

TABLE II: PERCEPTIONS OF LEADERSHIP BEHAVIOR

Percentage believing the leadership wants:

Rate of Participation	What the Average Teacher Wants	What the Influential Teachers Want	What the Administrators Want	What the Leadership Thinks	Don't Know
Low					
Males	17	21	31	15	16
Females	25	18	19	14	24
Moderate					
Males	20	22	32	14	12
Females	32	24	11	18	15
High					
Males	45	18	13	8	14
Females	55	10	7	21	7

seen in a tabulation (Table II) of members' perceptions of the distribution of influence within the organization. In a way, this table elucidates the various political philosophies of the members. Those who believe that the leadership responds to the desires of the Average Teacher are the pluralists of the organization—they reflect the optimistic belief that the majority rules in fact as well as in theory. Those who think that the Influential Teachers are the people to whom the leadership turns are the patricians, who believe that only a few influentials are able to exert power. Those who think that the leadership is responsive more to the demands of school administrators than of teachers represent an elite theory unique to teachers' organizations which will be discussed more thoroughly at a later point. One might call this the "theory of an administrative conspiracy." Those who believe that the leaders of the organization do only what the leadership itself thinks best are the autocrats of the teaching profession.

Numerically, women are, in general, the pluralists, men the patricians. Most women believe that Average Teachers are the major reference group for the leadership. Except for the most active group (a minority of men), men tend to believe that Influential Teachers and especially administrators have more to say than Average Teachers do.

THE PROBLEM OF ADMINISTRATIVE DOMINANCE

The question of administrators controlling the organization is particularly acute. In any organization cohesion is maximized as the homogeneity of the group increases. As one seeks out the reasons for the breakdown of cohesion in organizations the most frequently encountered probable cause is a conflict between intragroup elements whose identification with the over-all category around which the group is organized is challenged by a sub-group identification. The greater the population which an organization attempts to embrace within its membership, the more likely that organization is to fall prey to internal conflict. Within every group the shared attitudes that are the basis of group activity can be cut into smaller patterns of attitudes. An attempt to build a large organization including all possible segments of an occupation runs the risk of increasing heterogeneity and hence internal conflict.

The fact that both school administrators and teachers belong to educational associations is one of the major points of conflict between teachers associations and unions. The union point of view is that any organization that contains both administrators and teachers cannot be responsive to the needs of the teachers. They argue that administrators usually have the power to hire and fire teachers, to promote them and give them tenure; in general, to control their occupational fortunes. Consequently, they argue, teachers can hardly be expected to gain redress through an organization which puts them in face-to-face confrontation with those who are the source of the grievances. The unions point out that not only do administrators make more money than teachers, they are also frequently reimbursed for certain professional expenses. In the educational system administrators have more power than teachers, and to place administrators with teachers in one and the same organization is only to further consolidate their control over teachers.

The domination of teachers organizations by school administrators was largely responsible for the formation of the American Federation of Teachers, a union that excludes superintendents from its membership. Teachers associations are not unaware of union attacks upon them but they deny that the inclusion of teachers and administrators in one and the same organization results in administrative dominance. A typical association position on this matter emerged from the 1966 electoral struggle in Portland, Oregon between the union and NEA. On the question of administrative dominance, the NEA's representative said:

> Our organization includes teachers, supervisors, and administrators because they all have one common goal—better education for the children. The union teacher groups have only teachers as members and I believe that driving this wedge between educational ranks is harmful to education in general.[13]

The union, on the other hand, believes that it was able to make inroads into association membership because,

> The Oregon Educational Association is kind of a company union dominated by administrators and supervisors. Our group is made up strictly of teachers and we intend to attract the career teachers because we exercise a more militant voice in behalf of the teachers.[14]

[13] *Portland Oregonian,* January 23, 1966, p. 26.
[14] *Ibid.*

The pleas for unity on the part of educational associations do not diminish the fact that for male teachers the problem of administrative dominance is very real. Administrative dominance is not reduced substantially by the establishment in the associations of classroom-teacher subgroups from which administrators are excluded. Female teachers trust administrators but males distrust them, not only within the organization but generally within the educational system. For example, 14 per cent of the female teachers responding to an NEA poll [15] listed administrators as sources of professional encouragement, but only eight per cent of the male teachers so responded. Another NEA study[16] showed that more male than female teachers felt that a lack of strong support of teachers by school principals was responsible for disciplinary problems in the classroom. Some of the tension between the male teachers and administrators may be a consequence of the fact that administrators represent a position to which male teachers aspire. To women, by contrast, administrators do not represent a competitive threat. It is apparent, therefore, that the strategy of unions in emphasizing administrative dominance in teachers associations is well attuned to the anxieties of male teachers.

The lack of resentment among female teachers for administrators within the organization may be less a result of the absence of competition than of the tendency of females by nature to be more trusting than males of authority. Their trust of authority is suggested by the distribution of those teachers who believe that the leaders do what the leadership thinks best. This question is an alienated alternative; that is, it is assumed that teachers who selected this alternative used it as an instrument to indicate some dissatisfaction with the organization. Men apparently did not similarly use it, for the percentage of male teachers choosing this alternative decreases as their activity rate increases. Active males being the least dissatisfied with the organization, the fact that few of them selected this alternative supports the assumption that this is an alienated response. For women, the opposite pattern develops: as their activity increases, the percentage of female teachers choosing

---

[15] National Education Association, *The American Public School Teacher,* 1960-61 (NEA, April, 1963), p. 69.

[16] National Education Association, *Student Behavior in Secondary Schools* (NEA, August, 1965), p. 27.

this alternative also increases. Women being much more satisfied with the organization than men, one can only assume that for them this is *not* an alienated response. Female teachers apparently approve of a leadership that does not hold itself responsible to the desires of the members. This approval may reflect a generally docile attitude on the part of women. Either they do not expect as much democracy within an organization as do men or they have so much confidence in their leadership that they believe that it can provide virtual representation without the necessity for actual representation.

ACCURACY OF INFORMATION
ABOUT POLICY POSITIONS

How well and truly informed are members about the policy positions of their organization? Male teachers take a less active role in the organization and read less organizational literature than female teachers do, yet about 33 per cent of them are able to identify correctly the policy positions of their organizations. In contrast only about 15 per cent of the female members have any knowledge of the policy positions of their organization. Even among the most active members about twice as many men as women were able to give "correct" answers. It seems clear, therefore, that although women are satisfied and docile, they are not especially well informed about the activities of the organization. On the other hand men, who are neither satisfied nor very active in the organization, actually are better informed about it.

Small-town teachers are the bulwark of the educational association in terms both of supportive values and rate of participation. For them, active participation *does* lead to a knowledge of the policy positions of the organization. Small-town teachers are more likely than big-city teachers to identify correctly the positions of the organization. Active participants in an organization are more exposed to the literature of the organization and accordingly may be expected to have more information about the behavior of the organization. That women do not can be taken as evidence of their inability or unwillingness to subject the organization to a critical evaluation.

It is curious that women—the most active, least satisfied members —are the best informed about what the organization is doing. Being more satisfied with their jobs, perhaps women are also more satisfied to go along with their educational association without really caring very much about its public positions. Their participation appears to be less critical participation than supportive activity, perhaps motivated as much by a desire to be as professional as possible as by a desire to meet and talk with other teachers; but not out of any desire to get bogged down in difficult problems of public education.

THE SMALL TOWN TEACHER AND
THE EDUCATIONAL ASSOCIATION

Small-town teachers are more active in teachers associations than are teachers in large cities, but small-town teachers participate substantially less in the general political process; moreover, their perceptions of the proper role in this process are much more restrained than those of large-city teachers. Urban environment seems to produce a stronger political orientation among teachers as well as other citizens. Conflict situations are more likely to arise in heterogeneous, densely populated areas, and the perceptions of small-town teachers reflect the relative political quiescence of small-town life. This reflection is carried over into the classroom. Small-town teachers talk in this classrooms about politics far less than do teachers in large cities in their classrooms. In spite of their over-all political quiescence, small-town teachers take just as active a part in local public school politics as do large-city teachers.

Although they take a more active role in the formal affairs of the organization small-town teachers are not very likely to have personal contacts with its leaders. Their pattern of participation is structured almost entirely along formal lines. Enthusiasm for educational associations runs high in small towns. Small-town teachers are generally cynical about political and social life, yet they are extremely happy with the professional organization and are more likely to declare themselves in substantial agreement with organization policies than are large-city teachers.

It is curious that small-town teachers are considerably less likely to believe that administrators dominate teachers associations, yet the evidence is that administrative control of educational associations is much greater in small towns, where antiunion sentiment is very intense. Perhaps small-town teachers see administration participation not as a matter of control but rather as a matter of unity of interest. The model teacher, if we take educational association's definition, is the small-town teacher. Small-town teachers are satisfied with every aspect of the association's performance, and they display this satisfaction with almost filial devotion. Outside the big cities the educational association can do no wrong.

In the big cities, the educational associations are losing the confidence of the teachers. The unions are gaining influence in the cities while educational associations are maintaining or increasing their influence in the small towns. But small-town teachers are a minority of association membership, and ultimately the educational associations will have to revise their traditional appeals.

Small-town teachers are not politically motivated and their distrust of politics keeps them reticent and restrained. Their distrust of things radical colors their perception of the proper role of the educational association. Small town teachers seem to be far more professionalistic than their big-city counterparts; for example, they are avid readers of the professional journals and indicate themselves substantially more satisfied with the content. It is typical of big-city teachers with more sophisticated and critical views to regard the publications of teachers associations as just so much irrelevant propaganda, but small-town teachers accept the official line uncritically, even gratefully. Small-town teachers like the associations as they are and want to keep them out of politics, especially electoral politics, whether or not educational issues are involved. Few of them— about one-fourth—believe that their association endorses political candidates, whereas a majority of big-city teachers believe that educational associations do endorse candidates, although not regularly, openly, or vigorously. It is true that educational associations, perhaps in response to the threat of unions, have given serious consideration to sustaining electoral programs, but even if the associations wanted to become more politically involved in small towns, the severe negative reaction of the teachers might prevent them from doing so.

THE RECRUITMENT OF LEADERS

A curious aspect of the behavior of women teachers is their failure to dominate the formal office-holding structure of teachers associations. Very few teachers have ever been officers of their state association; probably fewer than 10 per cent of the teachers hold office during their teaching careers. However, state organizations are divided into local units which hold charters from the main body, and in these local teachers organizations leadership positions are much easier to acquire. About one third of the members of these local organizations have at one time held local office. Local teachers associations are considerably more popular with teachers than are state organizations, perhaps because they are the grass roots organizations. Locals are regarded as less likely to be dominated by administrators and the belief is strong that the average member is the most influential reference group for local leadership. This may well be true because it does not cost any money to become active in a local and average teachers can also afford to spend time in local activities.

Local organizations seem to recruit more leaders from among the inexperienced teachers than do the state organizations. About 20 per cent of the members who have been teaching less than two years have been local officers; less than 1 per cent have held office in a state organization. A majority of teachers who have taught nine or more years have been officers of the local organization, whereas only about one-fourth of this group have held office in the state association.

State and local associations generate more enthusiasm and participation among women than among men, yet the leaders of both are more likely to be male teachers from small towns. Why is it that women, who are substantially more active than men in the organization, do not hold formal leadership positions in proportion to their activity? Male prejudice against allowing women to hold positions of formal authority may be a factor. Male teachers are reluctant to work under female principals and, as a general rule, it appears that organizations function best when women are placed in positions of authority only over other women. Do male members of the educational associations likewise find it impossible to tolerate female leadership even though they do not wish to involve themselves very deeply in the affairs of the organization? If this is so, they might exercise their voting privilege to keep women away from authority positions. In some states, tensions between men and women have been resolved by the practice of rotating the presidency of the state organization annually between a man and a woman. Teachers associations acknowledge that males and females have fundamentally different values, but they have not made any appreciable effort to improve their image among men, especially among the young, urban male teachers who are leading the revolt against the educational associations and whose only goal is to raise teachers' salaries without concern for the unprofessional aspects of union activity.

THE INFLUENCE OF THE ORGANIZATION UPON THE VALUES OF ITS MEMBERS

What is the effect of group membership upon the political values and attitudes of the members? To what extent is the membership of an interest group willing to accept its leadership's recommendations on questions of public policy? Many interest groups such as the National Association of Manufacturers, American Medical Association, and the AFL-CIO vigorously involve themselves with public issues and political candidates, and seek to influence their memberships through propaganda. The effect an organization has upon members' attitudes and behaviors is exerted through interpersonal interactions as well as through formal expressions of opinion in media such as magazines and bulletins. The organization is only one of a number of competing demands upon the values and behaviors of the members. For some members, the demands of the organization will be sufficiently strong to outweigh all others. Other members will be more influenced by other sources of demand; their family obligations, for instance. Obviously, then not all members are equally vulnerable to group appeal. Some kinds of appeal are more effective than others. When members fail to perceive the relevance of the group's position to their personal well being, they are less likely to support the group's position. Presumably, members of educational associations are most responsive to appeals that directly involve their status as teachers, but there are undoubtedly some members of these organizations who accept the leadership's position uncritically irrespective of the issue. It is a well documented fact of communications research that the source of a communication is a determinant of its persuasive efficacy. In Klapper's words,

> The source of a communication ought to be more exact, the source as conceived by the audience has been shown to influence the persuasive efficacy of a communication itself. In general, sources which the audience hold in high esteem appear to facilitate persuasion, while sources which the audience holds in low esteem appear to constitute at least a temporary handicap. The possible base of such esteem are perhaps infinitely variable. Audiences have been shown, for example, to respond particularly well to specific sources because they consider them of high prestige, highly credible, expert, trustworthy, close to themselves, or just plain likeable.[17]

It is a common assumption that large interest groups, such as teachers associations, are politically powerful because they can control the voting behavior of large numbers of people. But merely having a large membership does not automatically mean that this membership is subject to organizational influence. In some cases, no effort by the organization is really necessary to inform the membership about the "right" position to take. As Stokes puts it, "Wheat farmers may respond in unison to a drop in the price of their crop without needing a formal organization to tell them that their pocketbook nerve has been touched."[18] It might be true that, where members of a particular occupational group are well aware that they are suffering, only an organization could channel their anxiety toward accomplishment of a specific goal. The main thrust of the evidence about the influence of organizations upon their membership, however, is that the ability to deliver a bloc vote is considerably less than the leaders of organizations would like to believe. Accordingly, we should expect that small town teachers and women teachers should be more likely to follow the dictates of the organization than large town teachers and men.

[17] Joseph T. Klapper, *The Effects of Mass Communication* (New York: The Free Press of Glencoe, Inc., 1960), p. 99.
[18] Donald E. Stokes, *Voting Research and the Businessman in Politics* (Ann Arbor: The Foundation for Research on Human Behavior, 1960), p. 15.

We should also expect that people who have held formal office in an educational association (and who are as expected much more satisfied with the organization than teachers who have never been elected to an office) would be more likely to follow its lead. Another factor which should contribute to the impact of the organization upon its membership is the extent to which its membership sees the purpose of the organization as political. Those who believe that the organization should not engage in politics would be less likely to follow its suggestions than those who think its proper function can be found within the political process. We would expect, therefore, a relationship between an individual's perception of the political role of the organization and his willingness to follow its advice.

Unfortunately, the issues are not exactly clear-cut, for we find certain contradictory elements present. Consider for example, small town teachers who attribute great prestige to the organization and hence, according to the first theory, should be expected to follow its advice. Yet they assign a relatively low political function to it and, according to the second theory, would be disinclined to follow its advice.

The effect of an organization upon certain values is sometimes quite subtle. Does a member who is willing to follow the explicit political suggestions of the organization—for example, its endorsement of a candidate—necessarily share the organization's political philosophy as it is articulated by the leadership? Consider the attitude of teachers toward unions. As teachers become more experienced, their distrust of unions increases; as teachers increase their activity in the organization their distrust of unions increases. Active teachers are often experienced teachers. How, then, can we determine whether activity in the organization predisposes a member to distrust unions, or whether this distrust of unions is a natural consequence of an increasing teaching experience? To explore such problems one must first ascertain the extent to which members are ready to accept the suggestions of an organization and the extent to which the values of members are in accordance with those of the organization. It is essential to keep in mind the influence of the extent to which the values expressed by the organization are perceived by members to be related to proper activities of the organization as defined by the members. Thus, just as we would expect doctors to be more sympathetic to AMA appeals about Medicare, we would expect teachers to be more sympathetic to appeals from their organization about educational matters.

Educational associations typically are involved only in a very limited way with the political process, hence the question of the probable effects of their political advice is somewhat hypothetical. Yet, if educational associations are to respond to the threat of union competition they will have to become more political. Presumably, teachers who want the organization to involve itself in political affairs will be likely to value the guidance of the organization if it does so. The relationship between the perception of the proper political role of the organization and members' willingness to accept its guidance need not be very close with respect to educational matters. Suppose, for example, an educational association endorses a political candidate or takes a stand on a public issue. In this case there is a clear relationship between what the membership perceives to be the legitimate political role of the organization and their willingness to follow the leadership of the organization: the stronger the political role perceived for the organization, the more likely the membership is to follow the leadership's suggestion. Suppose an educational association advocates support of an issue directly related to education; say, the question of a state sales tax to benefit the public schools. Because many teachers believe that this is the sort of thing that educational associations ought to be involved in there need be much relationship between one's perception of the political role of the organization and his willingness to follow its suggestions. Because teachers make a clear distinction between professional educational matters and political matters, most of them would probably go along with the organization's recommendation on this issue irrespective of what they thought it should be doing in the electoral process.

There is, in fact, almost no relationship between the willingness of members to accept the guidance of their organization on educational matters and their perception of the proper political role of the organization. Most teachers eschew an active political role for the organization, yet many of them would follow its advice if advice was forthcoming only on educational matters; more teachers would be influenced by the organization in educational than in political affairs. Even on educational issues, however, the majority of teachers would not necessarily go along with the advice of the teachers association. In terms of the total number of people a teachers association could persuade to adopt a given point of view, the association's impact is not very great. On political questions it is only among those who advocate a very active political role for the organization that there is a consensus that the voice of the organization ought to be heeded. But the teachers who want teachers associations to involve themselves heavily in politics are only a small minority of the total teaching population, hence the effect of teachers association recommendations on political matters is relatively minute.

The establishment of a relationship between members' perceptions of the proper political role of their organization and their willingness to follow its political advice suggests that the best clue to understanding members' susceptibility to organizational persuasion is in the definition of proper organization role, not credibility of source. This conclusion is not entirely correct, however. Small-town teachers are the least politically oriented of all the organization, yet they are considerably more likely than big-city teachers to follow the organization's lead. For example, even small-town teachers are violent in their disapproval of the involvement of educational associations in education politics, the majority of them would accept its guidance. The behavior of small-town teachers, however, is probably an exception that proves the rule, for they are so totally uncritical of the organization in all matters—just about anything it does is all right with them. They impute extreme reliability to the source of the recommendations, a predilection that outweighs their general political negativism.

The conclusion that credibility of source is not so important can be shown by examining the behavior of men and women. Assuming that the more active members of the educational association are the more willing to accept its leadership, and because activity is related to satisfaction with the organization, there is the presumption that women would be more likely to accept organizational guidance than men. The influence of the organization on its members as individuals varies directly with the activity rate of an individual, but on political issues men at every level of activity are more likely to accept the leadership of the organization than women are. Even though they distrust the organization, are cynical about the behavior of its leaders, and disagree with many of its goals, men are more willing to accept its political advice. Teachers associations rarely give political advice, but what a reservoir of strength they could tap if they would offer to men, who want a vigorous political organization, a much more active political role than they now exercise. In maintaining an aloofness from the electoral process, teachers associations are passing up a very valuable political resource: people.

The potential influence of the teachers association on educational matters bears little relationship to its influence in political affairs. For female teachers, willingness to accept organizational leadership *increases* on educational matters with activity; for males, willingness to accept such guidance *decreases* with activity. On questions involving education, women, who are the most satisfied with and the most active in teacher associations, are more likely to follow organizational guidance. On political issues, an organizational concern that men find more attractive than women, it is men who are most disgruntled and dissatisfied members, those most likely to accept political guidance from the educational association.

These reactions appear more related to the definitions respectively of males and females of what the organization is than to male-female levels of satisfaction with the organization. Female teachers are more anxious than male teachers that the organization declare itself on educational matters, and they are more willing to follow its advice when it does so. Male teachers want the organization to extend its competence to the general political arena and would be willing to follow its advice would it do so.

It is possible that female teachers are less willing to follow the political advice of the organization because they are being cross-pressured by another source. Presumably, the most severe cross pressures upon female teachers are from their husbands. The evidence suggests that conflict over political matters between husband and wife usually results in the wife being persuaded to accept her husband's point of view. It is likely at any rate that the family is a more important reference group for most women than is a professional organization: a woman is likelier to seek and heed political advice from her husband than from her organization. Unmarried women presumably would be more inclined than married women to follow the position of the organization.

There is some evidence to support this possibility but, in the overview, the conclusion that men will follow the political advice of the organization because they want it to *be* a political organization is not shaken. This conclusion is based on the following observations. At both the inactive and moderately active levels married women are more likely to accept the leadership of the organization than are single women. At the very active level, however, the situation is reversed and single women become considerably more amenable to organizational suggestions than do married women. On educational issues this difference is not very great but on political questions the difference between single and married women is substantial. Therefore on educational matters, about which women agree the organization has a more legitimate right to speak than it does on political matters, the influence of the organization is roughly comparable among single and married women. It is only on questions of politics that the influence of the organization becomes much more extreme among single women, and it is only among the very active women that this difference exists. Consequently, even if we factor out married women and examine only single ones it is still true that men are more likely than women to accept the political guidance of the organization. All in all, therefore, it is probable that, whereas credibility of source is important as a contributor to the persuasive effects of organizational communications, the more important determinant of the extent to which an organization can exercise influence over its members is the perception that the members have a legitimate function of the organization.

This discussion has dealt with what is essentially a hypothetical situation. From this discussion we have been able to predict the probable success of an extension of educational associations into the electoral process. To examine the actual rather than the hypothetical impact of the organization upon ideology, let us return once again to the case of the unions. Teachers organizations have emphasized very clearly their antipathy towards unions, contrasting their own professionalism with what they criticize as the working class intellectual assumptions of unions. Unionism, they argue, destroys professionalism; union tactics generally but particularly strikes are bad for a professional image and must be discouraged. As an NEA leader recently remarked, "we don't believe in the muscle side of it—teacher strikes as encouraged by the union leaders." Antiunionism is an official ideology of teachers associations, and those who are the most active in the associations generally are the most hostile toward unions. But it is also true that those who are the most active in nonorganizational politics are considerably *less* hostile toward unions. Consequently, there seems to be at least a presumption that teachers associations instill in their members the antiunion line. It is reasonable to assume that the more active a person is within an organization the more likely he is to express an opinion in conformity with the official ideology.

This relationship cannot be established, however, solely on the basis of the fact that about twice as many active members of associations are opposed to unions in comparison to the inactive members. Longevity of teaching experience alone, irrespective of organizational participation, reduces the enthusiasm of teachers for unions and strikes. This trend is in accordance with the greater political conservatism and quiescence of the more experienced teachers. Therefore it may be true that, even if there were no organization providing antiunion propaganda, the willingness of teachers to support union activities would decline. Whereas the increasing political conservatism of teachers would certainly reduce their sympathy toward unions, the continual antiunion propaganda on the part of educational associations probably strengthens and magnifies this process.

Consider, for example, the readership of the professional association magazines. Among younger teachers, the difference between the attitudes of readers and nonreaders of official publications toward unions is not very great—about one-third of both groups are sympathetic to unions. Among experienced teachers, however, about one-third of the nonreaders remain sympathetic to unions, but among readers only one-sixth are union sympathizers. This suggests the possibility that the effect of organizational antiunion propaganda is long-term, that its full potential is realized only over a period of several years.

Male teachers display a strong determination to resist the official organization line. On educational matters, women are more susceptible to organizational appeals than men but on the question of unions, which is perhaps *the* issue among public school personnel, women are more likely to possess the official ideology, and activity within the organization strengthens and reinforces "professional" orientations. Among organizationally inactive teachers, about 33 per cent of the males and only a slightly lower percentage of the females are sympathetic to unions. About 33 per cent of the active male teachers are union sympathizers but only 3 per cent of the active females indicate any substantial identification with union goals. So, although women are slightly more, perhaps by nature, opposed to strikes, the gap between the sexes increases enormously as involvement in the organization increases. Women are not especially well informed about most of the affairs of the organization, hence the fact that they get the official message about unions is some indication of the intensity with which this message is communicated.

CONCLUSIONS

Male teachers, whose alienation from the educational system is great, find no succor in teachers associations. Far from being a mechanism through which the system might be changed, teachers associations function as agents for the preservation of the *status quo*. They do not reflect the ideology of male teachers, they draw little support from among male teachers. We have seen, however, that if they chose to do so, teachers associations could probably mobilize the male high school teachers. As it is, however, teachers associations are the representatives principally of small-town female teachers, whereas high school teaching is becoming more and more an urban male occupation.

There are several possible alternative ways of resolving this dilemma of the failure of educational associations to represent the values of many of their members. All of them involve substantial adaptation of the teacher associations to the needs of the younger male teachers. One possibility is to segregate elementary teachers into separate organizations so that recognition would be given to the majority position of males in high school teaching and the minority position of males in elementary teaching. Coupled with this, if teachers associations become more militant and abandon their opposition to union methods they might be able to draw more support from among males. However, if things remain as they are, the dominant position of teachers associations in contrast to unions seems bound to decline. Schools of education are probably only slightly less sympathetic to unions than is the National Education Association, yet in consequence of the recruitment of males into the profession they fill the profession with teachers to whom the appeals of unions are greatest.

Chapter Four:
POLITICS
AND
THE CLASSROOM

The general public is less concerned with the internal structure and functioning of the schools than they are with the product of educational systems: the students. The educational system is both a conscious and unconscious agent of political socialization. Teachers, as those representatives of the educational system who have the most frequent personal contacts with students, function as communication agents for the total educational system, which in turn reflects values of the society. Exactly how great an impact the educational system has upon the political values of students is an unsettled question and is not the central problem of this chapter. We may proceed on the premise that the educational system serves to "indoctrinate the upcoming generation with the basic outlooks and values of the political order." [1] The educational system operates in competition with other agents of political socialization, among them the primary group and mass media. There is no way to measure accurately the relative contributions of each agent to the total socialization of a member of society, but whatever the impact of the educational system upon values may be, society assumes it to be great. As Easton puts it:

In our society at any rate, schools get the child from at least the age of five and hold him, with certain differences for class origins and state legislations, until fifteen or sixteen. In that period the schools occupy an increasing portion of the child's and adolescent's day. If for no other reason than that the time at the disposal of educational institutions at this impressionable stage of development is so great,

[1] V. O. Key, Jr. *Public Opinion and American Democracy* (New York: Alfred A. Knopf, 1961), p. 316.

we might expect the impact of political orientations to be of equivalent force.[2]

The architects of political systems who have given the matter any thought reach much the same conclusions. To quote Key:

> One of the first tasks of new rulers has been to rewrite the textbooks and to purge the school system of adherence to old ways in order that memories of the old society might be erased and that the educational machine might be used to imprint the goals of the new order upon the plastic minds of the youth of the land.[3]

The extent to which educational institutions act as conscious impregnators of the minds of the youth varies from time to time and country to country. Bessie Pierce described American schools of the 1920's as chauvinistic propagandists for conservatism and the *status quo*.[4] Today chauvinism is not apparent, at least in textbooks, but there is an emphasis upon what Litt calls the democratic creed, which emphasizes student participation in the political process.[5] In an analysis of history textbooks, Alexander observes that textbooks are cultural products of their time and finds that contemporary textbooks focus on "optimism, which derives from much of the values of the promotional age we live in." [6]

Perhaps it is a decline in chauvinism that has drawn down upon schools the wrath of radical conservatives. If the purpose of textbooks and classroom instruction is something more than the indoctrination of youth with overt ideologies, then indeed the schools are not performing the functions that the radical right imputes as proper to them. But if the object of education is the training of youth for participation in a democratic society, political liberals will find little comfort in the optimistic and uncritical nature of text-

[2] David Easton, "The Function of Education in a Political System," *The School Review* (Autumn 1957), p. 314.

[3] Key, *loc. cit.*

[4] Bessie L. Pierce, *Public Opinion and the Teaching of History in the United States, op. cit.; Civic Attitudes in American School Textbooks* (Chicago: University of Chicago Press, 1930).

[5] Edgar Litt, "Civic Education, Community Norms, and Political Indoctrination; *American Sociological Review*, 28 (February, 1963), pp. 69-75.

[6] Albert Alexander, "The Gray Flannel Cover on the American History Textbook," *Social Education*, 24 (January 1960), pp. 11-14.

books. If textbooks are becoming bland and devoid of value it does not necessarily follow that teachers are, too. After all, it is a relatively simple matter for a teacher to augment the more or less objective nature of a textbook with personal values.

How do teachers see their role in class? What are they teaching for? Do they make a distinction between facts and values? Do they advocate particular points of view, or do they merely "referee" and retain their objectivity? How much is politics talked about in class? These are some of the questions this chapter will entertain.

We know something about what students think ought to happen in class, but very little about what teachers think should happen. We learn from the Purdue University studies of American teenage opinion that more than one half of the nation's high school students believe that teachers should express personal opinions and judgments about the American political and economic systems:

> Pupils evidently not only want to learn *facts* about a subject, but also want *values* put on these facts, even when this invades controversial areas.[7]

Most teenagers also believe that teachers should be free to criticize our form of government and economic system. As the consumers of the classroom experience, therefore, students want this experience to emphasize controversy.

Do teachers share with the students this perception of the classroom as an arena of controversy? Do teachers have to reconcile two roles—one as teacher, the other as citizen? That is to say, do teachers express one political value to adults in the community but a different value to students in the classroom? On each kind of activity there are some restraining elements. The teacher's life is always fit subject for public scrutiny. The goldfish-bowl situation of teachers may hinder them from being as active politically as citizens who are not public servants. The fact that they deal with youngsters may be a similarly inhibiting factor—people seem to think that, up to a certain age, youth's sense of idealism should remain pure. There is even some sentiment that youth ought to be conscientiously taught

---

[7] H. H. Remmers and D. H. Radler, *The American Teenager* (Indianapolis: Bobbs-Merrill Company, Inc., 1957), p. 125.

to believe that the world is a bit more perfect and free of conflict than it actually is. The argument runs that youth should be brought to believe that the American system of government is the most perfect yet devised by man. The more unpleasant aspects of our society can be set aside for later.

American high schools do not inform their students of the realities of the political process. Believing, as most of them do, that all is right with the world students exposed in college to a more realistic interpretation of American politics are sometimes shocked into an unnecessarily extreme pessimism. Many students have said that college courses in American government have so shaken their idealism that they no longer think political participation is necessary or desirable.

Edgar Litt's study in the Boston metropolitan area examined the civic training of youth in upper-, middle-, and lower-class communities.[8] In the upper-class community, the textbooks used and the manner in which the course was taught emphasized participation as a responsibility of citizenship. Participation was emphasized, if somewhat less vigorously, in the middle-class community, substantially less in the lower-class community. The political alienation of lower-class citizens may, therefore, be reflected in the classroom experience of lower-class youths. Litt found that only in the upper-class community was there any significant effort to teach the realities of the political process, and how political power and group conflict are essential and natural ingredients of political life. In the middle- and lower-class communities, politics was presented as a "formal mechanistic set of governmental institutions with emphasis on its harmonious legitimate nature rather than as a vehicle for group struggle and change." [9] Except for the upper-class community, the civic training given to youth did not equip them to come to grips with the real world of politics and may have contributed to the substantial decline of idealism that is typical of the freshman year of college experience. It may well be that teachers function simply more as promulgators of societal myths than as critical examiners of the political process.

[8] Litt, *op. cit.*
[9] Edgar Litt, *op. cit.*, p. 73.

INTRA–CLASS VERSUS EXTRA–CLASS EXPRESSION OF OPINIONS

Community pressure upon the behavior of teachers apparently is not as oppressive as once was thought, but the sentiment is still fairly strong that the proper place for the expression of political opinions by teachers is away from the impressionable minds of the children. Teachers were asked to examine a list of behaviors and to indicate which of the behaviors they thought it was proper for them to undertake. Beside each activity in the following list is indicated the percentage of teachers who believed the activity a proper one for them to engage in:

1. Joining a political party (93 per cent);
2. Serving as a precinct worker (91 per cent);
3. Running for a political office (88 per cent);
4. Making a speech for a Presidential candidate outside school time (85 per cent);
5. Joining the Congress of Racial Equality (CORE) or the National Association for the Advancement of Colored People (NAACP) (82 per cent);
6. Joining a teachers union (71 per cent);
7. Publicly criticizing local government officials (58 per cent);
8. Taking part in CORE or NAACP demonstrations (43 per cent);
9. Going on strike to secure higher salaries or other benefits (29 per cent).

The majority of the teachers indicated belief that seven out of nine behaviors are proper. These teachers are relatively willing to involve themselves in community controversy.

These findings contrast with those of the NEA, which in a national survey found that only about one fifth of the teachers polled thought it proper for them to engage in the sort of local activities in our list.[10] A similar study of Wisconsin teachers indicated substantial teacher apprehension about engaging in community politi-

[10] National Education Association, *Research Bulletin,* 35 (1957), 34.

cal activity.[11] Both of these studies were made in 1956. It is possible that since that time teachers have been developing an increasing desire to express themselves. On the other hand, a difference in political culture may be evolving. Perhaps teachers' beliefs in the propriety of a given political act vary directly with their perceptions of the permissiveness of the communities in which they teach. Teachers were asked to rate the proprieties of a list of possible classroom behaviors, with the following results; a rather extreme contrast between the classroom and the community:

1. Speaking in favor of the United Nations (81 per cent);
2. Allowing an avowed atheist to address the class (58 per cent);
3. Speaking against the John Birch Society (48 per cent);
4. Speaking in favor of Medicare (47 per cent);
5. Allowing the distribution of anti-Communist literature published by the National Association of Manufacturers (46 per cent);
6. Defending the view that labor unions ought to be more closely regulated and controlled by the federal government (46 per cent);
7. Speaking against the censorship of books considered by some to be pornographic (43 per cent);
8. Speaking in favor of socialism (41 per cent);
9. Allowing the distribution of anti-Communist literature put out by the John Birch Society (31 per cent);
10. In a Presidential election, explaining to the class one's reasons for preferring a candidate (27 per cent).

It can readily be seen that teachers do not regard the classroom as a suitable forum for the expression by teachers of controversial opinions, or for that matter of noncontroversial opinions. In eight out of ten behaviors, a majority of teachers preferred noninvolvement.

Looking at classroom behavior as a whole, about 46 per cent of the teachers indicate that they should engage in expressive activity in class as compared with 71 per cent of the teachers taking an

---

[11] Lloyd V. Manwiller, "Expectations Regarding Teachers, *Journal of Experimental Education*, 26 (June, 1958), 316-54.

expressive position on extra class behaviors. As to expressing a personal opinion about a Presidential candidate to the class, these findings are in agreement with those of the NEA, which also found very few teachers willing to do this. It seems that teachers make a clear distinction between their behavior inside the classroom and their behavior within the community but outside the class.

Consider, for example, the behaviors relating to a Presidential election. In this case 85 per cent of the teachers think it proper for them to make a speech for a Presidential candidate outside of school, whereas only 27 per cent of them think it proper to do so within the classroom. It is clear that the United Nations is, for some reason, a legitimate topic upon which to express an opinion, but Medicare and socialism are not. The fact that these three behaviors all involve some dimension of the so-called liberal persuasion does not seem to be a distinguishing characteristic. In the first place, the proportion of teachers giving a positive response is cut by almost half when we omit the United Nations and consider Medicare and conservative behaviors are considered to be just about as improper as liberal ones.

The consensus that it is proper to speak out in favor of the United Nations may reflect the belief that this institution is sufficiently old and well established as to be a safe topic. Every other of the listed behaviors related to politics, whether liberal or conservative, is concerned with less well established institutions. Even allowing an atheist to address the class is regarded as more desirable than getting involved with anti-Communist literature or arguing for close federal regulation of labor unions. Atheism is not as much of a problem as political controversy. Politics in the classroom is clearly a very touchy subject. This is true probably because teachers perceive parents as being vigilant and suspicious about the political beliefs of teachers. Kent Jennings' survey of the attitudes of parents toward schools indicates this to be the case.[12] Inasmuch as the National Association of Manufacturers regularly makes its literature available to high schools, it is somewhat surprising that the teachers are so unwilling to accord this organization legitimacy. The NAM is not very welcome in the classroom, but it is regarded

[12] M. Kent Jennings, "Parental Grievances and School Politics" (paper presented to the Conference on Politics and Education, University of Oregon, June, 1966).

as a much more legitimate source of information than the John Birch Society.

Teachers apparently think it proper to join civil rights groups but not proper to demonstrate in support of the policies of these groups; proper to join a union, but not proper to go on strike. The worst thing a teacher can do, apparently, is make a declaration of personal preference for a Presidential candidate. On this point it is quite interesting to observe that the NEA found that teachers approve of holding a straw vote in class during a Presidential election, an activity that keeps a teacher's expression of his personal values at a minimum and is an approved technique of teaching children how to participate in politics as well. This is better than mere harmless behavior, it is a desirable behavior.

Teachers do not seem to want to make a very intense commitment to any position. If it is proper to join CORE or the NAACP, why is it improper to participate in the activities of these organizations if they involve public demonstrations? Why is such a distinction made between joining a union and taking part in a fairly conventional union activity? With regard to strikes, one cannot argue that striking among teachers is the same as striking among other workers. Public opposition to striking among teachers is undoubtedly greater than it would be if, say, members of the United Auto Workers elected to strike. Indeed, in some states teachers are forbidden by law both to strike and to honor picket lines. Granted the somewhat unique nature of this particular behavior, the fact that teachers also do not want to engage in racial demonstrations indicates that the opposition to the strike is not a unique consequence of the peculiar situation of education.

PROPER BEHAVIOR AND "SAFE" BEHAVIOR

Two criteria are involved in deciding questions of propriety: first, whether it is abstractly "right" for a teacher to engage in a certain activity; second, whether undertaking a specified course of action will provoke unfavorable reaction from those in a position to administer sanctions. Fear about the consequences of behavior may be related to perceptions of the propriety of behavior.

Let us test the hypothesis that proper behavior can be equated with "safe" behavior. A list of behaviors was submitted to teachers who were asked for their perceptions of how various groups or individuals within the community and within the school system might respond. The behaviors were then ranked according to the teachers' responses, and the resultant list compared with a list of the same behaviors ranked on the basis of propriety.

Table III ranks eight behaviors, ranked in order of propriety and

TABLE III: PROPER BEHAVIOR AND THE PERCEPTIONS
OF SANCTIONS

Rank in Order of Propriety	Behavior	Rank in Order of Fear of Sanctions
1	Speaking in favor of the United Nations	8
2	Allowing an atheist to address the class	4
3	Speaking against the John Birch Society	6
4	Speaking in favor of Medicare	7
5	Taking part in CORE or NAACP demonstrations	5
6	Speaking in favor of socialism	3
7	Going on strike	1
8	Explaining to the class one's preference of a Presidential candidate	2

r (Spearman's rank) = —.81

in order of the perceived likelihood of sanctions. It can readily be seen that *the greater the perception of probable sanctions, the less proper the behavior is perceived to be.* Speaking in favor of the United Nations is both proper and safe, but explaining to the class one's preference of Presidential candidate is both improper and unsafe. Teachers' perceptions of propriety are clearly pragmatic, not products of abstract choice or searching of conscience. This is not to say that teachers, deliberately or consciously, determine propriety exclusively on the basis of community response but it is quite apparent that estimations of probable consequences are part of the equation.

An alternative explanation of the reluctance of teachers to express themselves in class is, of course, that teachers are making a sharp distinction between facts and values, and that they view the classroom as a forum for the presentation of objective analyses rather than for the presentation of polemic arguments. This interpretation does not seem to be as valid as the one currently being pursued, however, because it does not explain the differences between the various kinds of possible behaviors. That is to say, if they truly were being objective, they would be as objective about Medicare as they are about the United Nations.

IDEOLOGICAL DIFFERENCES IN PERCEPTIONS OF THE CLASS: MALES AND FEMALES

Conservative teachers generally are more reluctant to express their values in class than are liberal teachers. Since men are more liberal than women, might it not be true that willingness to express opinions in class is really more closely related to ideology, and that the apparent association between expressive behavior and sex is spurious? But since men tend to be rebellious and dissatisfied with the educational system, and since it has been found that the expression of an opinion within the class is probably construed as undesirable, an alternative explanation is that men, whether they are liberal or conservative, want to express themselves in response to a psychological need to attack the system that is oppressing them.

Do males express their hostility by deviating from the established way of doing things? Or do conservatives, irrespective of sex, refrain from this activity as a general consequence of their more inhibited behavior? Consider the behavior ranked last in order of propriety— explaining to the class one's preference of Presidential candidate. As many men as women believe this behavior to be improper; but liberals think it more proper than conservatives do, and teachers with little experience think it more proper than teachers with more experience. So, whether they are men or women, liberals are expressive and conservatives are reticent. As a matter of fact, female liberals are slightly more likely to want to speak out for their Presidential candidate than are men. Ideology rather than sex appears to be the crucial determinant of a teacher's perception of the teacher's proper classroom role.

The relationship of ideology to perception of proper behavior on the above activity is interesting. The activity is obviously neither liberal nor conservative as are most of the others discussed at the beginning of the chapter. Yet even on a nonideologiacl question conservatives are substantially less expressive than are liberals. Conservatives, it appears, do not want to stimulate controversy in class even if the question is not biased, at least initially, one way or the other. Nevertheless, on every measure of classroom behavior, whether "conservative," "neutral," or "liberal," conservative teachers are less expressive. This is especially true of the older conservatives who undergo a radical reduction in expressive behavior.

The important point here is that both men and women react to potential political acts in roughly similar ways. Only ideology can discriminate between those teachers willing to express their opinions and those teachers preferring to remain silent. Why is it that men and women react to this problem in identical fashion? Is it, perhaps, because expressing an opinion about a Presidential candidate is the most severely disapproved behavior? In other words, since teachers in general feel this to be an especially reprehensible thing to do, the potential desire of men to strike back at the system is reduced because of the high probability of negative sanctions.

If this is true, it should also apply to the most dangerous type of extraclass behavior: going on strike. Here again the liberal teachers, whether they are men or women, are more prone to look upon the strike as a legitimate form of expression than are the conservative teachers. Teachers associations are able to instill strong antistrike sentiments among its more active members, but especially among females. Activity in associations seems to be the best clue to understanding the attitudes of teachers toward strikes, because the sex variable by itself does not seem to make very much difference. The differentiating quality of political ideology is probably related to the fact that conservatives find their values more in agreement with the educational association than do liberals. The essentially conservative and inhibiting effect of the educational association upon the behavior of teachers will be discussed later in the chapter.

Since we find no male-female differences upon the two kinds of behavior which are most threatening, the severity of these behaviors may obscure what appears to be a "normal" difference between men and women, thus leaving ideology free of sex differences. This seems to be the case, because on the other items liberals are more expressive than conservatives but male liberals are substantially more expressive than female liberals. Male conservatives are slightly more expressive than female conservatives. Take, for example, the delicate matter of speaking in favor of socialism, a "dangerous" doctrine. Women, especially those who have been teaching for a long time, irrespective of ideology, are not going to speak in favor of socialism. Men, and among them liberals more than conservatives, are more willing than women to talk about socialism.

Socialism is dangerous inasmuch as teachers believe that to talk about it is to invite attacks from the community. It ranks high on their list of sanction-producing behaviors, and their views probably reflect the fact that the charge of socialism in the schools is a favorite weapon of attacking organizations. Consider, for example, this statement by the American Medical Association:

> Many of our educators and many of the organizations to which they belong have for many years conducted an active, aggressive, campaign to indoctrinate their students in grammar school, high school, and college with the insidious and destructive tenets of the welfare state. This teaching of hatred and scorn for the American system of private enterprise has been so widespread and successful that as a result our voters are conditioned to accept all manner of totalitarian expedience in direct violation of economic law.[18]

Male liberals are also willing to express opinions in class in favor of Medicare which, according to the American Medical Association, is a concrete example of the drift towards socialism. However, teachers do not believe that speaking in favor of Medicare would produce as many sanctions as would speaking in favor of socialism. Teachers apparently fear more to discuss political philosophies than specific legislative programs. Male and female liberal teachers alike begin their teaching careers with considerable enthusiasm for the discussion of controversial topics in the class, but the enthusiasm of the females diminishes substantially while males persist in their expressive orientations. Women teachers thus give up their ideological commitments in favor of playing it safe, while men are more willing to take a chance. Whereas this distinction between men and women does not apply to the two most dangerous doctrines—going on strike and speaking in class in favor of a Presidential candidate—it does apply to behaviors only slightly less threatening.

[18] Cited in *Platform*, January, 1952, p. 5.

As we know, these differing functions are related to the ideologies of men and women teachers. Even on conservative issues, conservatives see less propriety in speaking out and using the classroom as a forum for the expression of values. Again, while it is obvious that ideology is related to expressive behavior on a particular item, it is equally obvious that conservatives are more reticent in their behavior patterns than are liberals, and that this reticence is not entirely owing to the extent to which their values are in harmony with a proposed behavior. It is true that conservatives are more willing to allow the expression of conservative than liberal beliefs, but on both sets of beliefs they are less expressive than liberals. However, these ideological differences are exaggerated when we consider males and females as separate teaching types. Two distinct patterns emerge: male liberals are expressive; female conservatives are reticent.

This relationship between sex, conservatism, and reticence is not exclusive to the classroom. The same pattern emerges within the community at large. Most community behaviors are not as threatening for teachers in general as are most classroom behaviors, conservatives are characterized by their reluctant attitudes. Just as in the classroom, in the direct political world there are certain kinds of potential acts which are more improper than others. Striking is taboo, but taking part in a racial demonstration is not quite so bad, especially among males. Females, however, apparently regard this sort of activity as especially reprehensible. The greater unwillingness of females to join racial demonstrations is related to the fact that such behavior is likely to produce a negative reaction. But it is not so dangerous as going on a strike, and males feel they can thus express themselves while incurring fewer sanctions than they might if they went on strike.

Teachers are more reluctant to express themselves in class than they are to express themselves in the community, but we can only speculate as to the reasons for this. Do they feel that the community is more willing to tolerate their behavior as citizens than teachers? Or do they, perhaps, feel that their values are more in harmony with those prevailing in the community than with those of the school administration? These questions relate both to the attitude of teachers toward the community and toward the school. Because the conservatives are the happiest with the educational system, it is difficult to believe that they would like to express themselves in class but are forced by a watchful administration to refrain. Likewise, their reluctance to express themselves outside of class is probably not due to any personal experience which caused them to lapse into quiescence.

Conservative teachers do not make as great a distinction between extraclass and intraclass behavior as do liberals. About 60 per cent of the liberals are expressive in extraclass activities compared to 49 per cent who are expressive in intraclass activities. About 43 per cent of the conservatives are expressive in extraclass activities compared to 38 per cent in intraclass activities. Conservatives are less expressive, but their classroom behavior does not appear to be very much different than their community behavior. The observation that teachers make a distinction between the classroom and the community is less applicable to conservatives than to liberals. For conservatives, expressive behavior is bad no matter what the arena; for liberals, the distinction between classroom and community is very real.

Conservative teachers apparently look upon their position within the educational establishment with more confidence. For example, we would presume that since teachers in small towns are more conservative than are teachers in large cities they would be the possessors of reticent role perceptions. This is the case with regard to such matters as unions and strikes, criticism of local officials and racial demonstrations, but it is not the case with regard to behavior within the classroom. There is practically no difference between the role perceptions of big-city and small-town teachers concerning expressive behavior within the classroom.

THE EFFECTS OF ORGANIZATIONAL AND POLITICAL PARTICIPATION

Another way of getting at the role perceptions of classroom teachers is to examine the socializing effects of organizational and political activity. Organizational participation reduces the tendency to agree with union objectives, and it may be that taking an active role in an educational association imbues teachers with the spirit of conformity even when professional association objectives are not involved. What about more general political participation? Political participation is to some extent a function of strongly felt partisan beliefs. The more strongly one believes in a partisan cause, the more likely he is to participate in politics; the more intense one's values, the more likely he is to feel the necessity to express these values. One would suppose that the more active a person is in the political process, then, the more willing he is likely to be to express his opinions both in the community and in the class. Thus, partisanship contributes to political activity, which strengthens partisanship, which in turn should produce a strongly expressive role orientation. People who regularly attend political meetings, give money to campaign funds, and are deeply concerned about the outcomes of elections should be so personally involved in public policy that they would find it practically impossible and certainly undesirable to be quiescent. To them, the role of good citizen would be defined as speaking out.

But would this expressive role necessarily obtain in the classroom, where there is some pressure to separate the citizen role from the teacher role? The answer is clear. In the classroom as much as within the community, active participants in the political process are substantially more expressive than are teachers who participate in elections and politics casually and less intensely.

The remarkable aspect of the effect of political activity upon expressive role orientations is that those who are active in the political process make practically no distinction whatsoever between extraclass and intraclass behavior. A majority of the active participants believe it is proper to express opinions in any situation. For those teachers who are inactive in the electoral process, on the other hand, the classroom imposes the usual barrier to expressive role orientations. Whereas 46 per cent of the inactives are expressive with regard to extraclass activities, only 37 per cent are expressive with regard to intraclass activities. Yet the percentage of expressive teachers among active teachers in this political process remains roughly the same for both categories of activity. For example, 76 per cent of the active teachers but only 46 per cent of the inactive teachers believe it is proper to publicly criticize local government officials. Fifty per cent of the active teachers but only 27 per cent of the inactive teachers believe that it is proper to speak in class in favor of socialism. Nearly 40 per cent of the active teachers but only about 20 per cent of the inactive teachers assume an expressive role orientation in the matter of explaining to the class one's preference of Presidential candidate.

Taking an active part in the political process is obviously related to a substantial reduction in reticence and to a desire on the part of the teacher to want to express his values and to create controversy within the class. Only about 9 per cent of the teachers are active in the electoral process; in terms of the gross impact of this activism upon the classroom situation, the consequences of the teachers' activity are slight. The substance of the controversy does not seem to make a great deal of difference—just about the same proportion of active teachers are willing to argue that labor unions should be regulated as are willing to speak in favor of nationalization of steel and railroads. Conservatives who are active participants in the political process are much more expressive than are the inactive conservatives in the articulation of both liberal and conservative beliefs. Active conservatives are not as expressive as active liberals, but activism in the political process, nevertheless, operates to mitigate some of the inhibiting effects of conservatism.

Does participation in the educational association produce an expressive teacher? It is clear that the basic motivation for participation in the political process is involvement in politics, but the motivations of those who are active in the educational association are not so clear. Most people who join an educational association don't do so out of political motivations; a substantial number join because they think they have to. Lane's survey of group influences upon political participation leads him to conclude that:

> There is another force at work which is quite independent of the political consciousness of friends and the organizations to which a person belongs. Isolation tends to make a person politically apathetic; group memberships in themselves increase his political interest and activity. This is true in the general sense that the more friends and organizational memberships a person has, the more likely he is to be asked his views on politics, regardless of the amount of information he has. He is more likely to vote if he has more organizational memberships, no matter where he is in the social system. And this is true

of relatively nonpolitical recreational groups as well as unions and business organizations.[14]

Following Lane's argument, we would expect that participation in the organization increases expressive role orientations even though this participation is not primarily politically motivated. Expressive behavior should increase because the active participants in the organization interact frequently with other people. They are not isolated, therefore they should be interested in politics. This interest in politics would make them more expressive if the theory held for the educational association, but it does not. The development of expressive or combative role orientations is not related in any way to active participation in the educational organization. In less than half the behaviors discussed in this chapter the more active members of the educational associations take a more expressive position. Furthermore, in most of the cases in which they do take a more expressive position, the difference between the active and the inactive members is negligible. It is just as likely that the active members of the association will be reticent in comparison with the passive members. Thus, considering intraclass behavior, 42 per cent of the active members and the same percentage of the inactive members are expressive. This contrasts sharply with the 54 per cent of the active participants in the electoral process who are expressive with regard to intraclass behavior. Also, the organizationally active teachers are *less* expressive with regard to extraclass behavior. The reticence of the active members is related to their vigorous opposition to unions. On the other hand, there is practically no difference between the active and inactive members of the association with regard to public criticism of local officials and taking part in CORE or NAACP demonstrations.

It is quite clear that there is a radical difference in the effects of the two kinds of activity upon teachers' perceptions of their political roles. In general, political participation contributes to expressivism but organizational participation contributes to reticence. Consider, for example, a comparison between the political actives and the organizational actives on the matter of public criticism of local

[14] Robert E. Lane, *Political Life* (New York: The Free Press of Glencoe, Inc., 1965), pp. 187-8.

officials. Seventy-six per cent of the politically active teachers believe this is proper compared to 60 per cent of the organizationally active teachers. Thus, not only does the organization inhibit behavior of teachers with regard to such clearly central topics as unions and strikes, it also inhibits behavior concerning what is an essentially public act: criticism of a local official.

It appears that the ideology of the organization as it is perceived by the active members is one of caution. It is true that among both active and passive teachers, a sort of peak of expressive behavior occurs among those with relatively few years of teaching experience, suggesting perhaps that expressive behavior is also a function of youth: as teachers become older they become less exuberant. Nevertheless, even when we consider teaching experience as a possible detractor from expressive behavior, the same over-all results emerge. The more experienced teachers are less expressive, but those who are active in the organization are considerably less expressive than those who are not active in the organization.

The educational association does not generate the same political interest among its members that other kinds of organizations do. The organization doesn't instruct its members to keep their mouths shut, but it is apparent that the official ideology of the organization, as it is perceived by those who are in a position to understand it best, is acceptance of things more or less as they are.

The effects of organizational activity and the effects of general political activity are exactly the opposite. Whether one regards the restraining effects of participation in an educational association as good or bad depends upon one's own personal values. Indeed, one point of view might be that the classroom should not be used as a forum for the expression of controversial ideas, because it should serve as a laboratory for objective analysis. This approach to the classroom is typical of college teachers. On the other hand, one might just as easily argue that it is important for high school children to be exposed to controversy in order to prepare them for their college experience and reduce the severity of the shock. Teachers who are active in the association are not going to lend their support to any activity which threatens the political system, but teachers who are active in the electoral process probably will do so. Even though the sorts of activities they engage in are well established and defined within the limits of the political system, the political actors are still more willing to tolerate behavior aimed at inducing a rapid change.

One looking within the teaching profession for potential recruits for the civil rights movement may as well stay away from the educational associations. Yet, even here, the question of right and wrong is dependent primarily upon how one views the legitimacy of racial protests. It is not the custom for social scientists to express personal values, but in this case the reader may as well know that I am disturbed about the effects of the educational association upon the attitudes of teachers. I would like high school students to learn about the real world of politics, not about the mythical world without problems and cleavages, if for no other reason than that it would greatly simplify the instructional task of the college instructor.

However, there is one aspect of the effects of organizational versus political participation which, it seems to me, transcends personal values. The interest group is supposed to buttress democratic society by stimulating participation. To function as a mediator between the society and the individual, the interest group must satisfy the demands of the individuals within it. To many individuals in the teaching profession the educational association is not personally satisfying; it is therefore not functional for them. The educational association is also dysfunctional for the society in that it does not encourage political participation or criticism of government officials. It is difficult to imagine a more fundamental requisite for democracy than the belief that government officials are as open to criticism as anyone else. Participation by teachers in the electoral process *strengthens* this belief. Participation by teachers in the organizational process *retards* this belief.

We commented upon some possible effects of the alienation and cynicism of teachers upon their ability to transmit to their students the responsibilities of democratic citizenship. These teachers are the rebels of the system. But what can we say of the active participants in the educational association who are the greatest supporters of the educational system? Since they are not conspicuous for belief in the validity of criticism of public officials, do they encourage political evaluation and expression on the part of their students? It may be that they are simply expressing the view that they, as teachers, should not criticize government officials, but that students (and anybody else) should do so. Yet even if this is true, the existence of a substantial body of people who think it inappropriate to be critical of government officials is disquieting.

Educational associations are, to some extent, dysfunctional for a healthy democratic society. It seems quite clear that the educational association stimulates neither a willingness to be critical nor a desire to participate. One cannot lay all the blame at the feet of the educational associations. Data collected by the NEA indicate that only about 57 per cent of the secondary school teachers believe it appropriate for them to work actively as members of political party organizations in state and national elections.[15] Thus teachers may shy away from political activity, but the effect of the educational association is certainly to intensify that inclination. The failure of the educational association to encourage political participation is probably not unrelated to the fact that according to the NEA about 60 per cent of the high school teachers feel restrained by the community against taking public positions on political issues. If the NEA had projected its inquiry a little bit further it would have found that the educational association is just as restraining, perhaps a bit more restraining than the community.

TALKING POLITICS IN CLASS

This discussion of role orientations shows us nothing about what goes on in the classroom. How much politics really gets talked about? We would assume that those who have expressive role orientations about classroom behavior also are inclined to talk about politics in class. A person's perception of what he ought to do quite often is at least a partial guide to what he actually does. For instance, there is a strong relationship between actual participation among teachers and expressive role orientations. There is also a relationship between expressive role orientations toward the classroom and actual discussion of political matters in class. If we examine the teachers who have a very low expressive behavior orientation, in contrast to those who have a very high expressive behavior orientation, we find that the amount of politics that is actually dis-

[15] NEA, *Research Bulletin,* 35 (1957), 61.

cussed in class varies considerably between the two. The more expressive the role orientation, the more often political discussion is undertaken with the class. About 33 per cent of the teachers whose attitude toward the classroom is expressive talk about political events in class as compared to about seven per cent of those whose attitude toward the class is one of quiescence.

However, the relationship between talking politics in class and possessing an expressive role orientation should not allow us to neglect a very essential aspect of the function of schools in the transmission of political values. The classroom is the very last place in which politics gets discussed. Expressive teachers are far more likely to talk about politics with their families and friends than they are with their classes. They are also more likely to talk about politics with other teachers, but not so likely as they are to talk about politics with their family and friends. Expressive teachers engage in this type of discussion far more than do the quiescent teachers, but the classroom is, in comparison to other arenas, relatively isolated from the political world. As we have noted, there is some tendency to believe that young minds must be kept free of doubt about the viability of the political system. Either the expressive teachers agree or they believe that those who have the authority to control their careers want to keep politics out of the classroom. Thus, in their actual behavior as well as their perceptions of propriety, teachers are able to make a distinction between community activity and classroom activity.

The relatively inhibiting nature of the classroom can be seen by the fact that almost 50 per cent of the expressive teachers have not only talked about politics, but have actually worked for candidates and attended political meetings, in comparison to about 14 per cent of the nonexpressive teachers. But even though they do talk about politics in class more than any other teachers, even for the expressive teachers the closing of the classroom door means goodbye to the world of politics.

What kinds of teachers do most of the talking about politics? Judging from what we have learned about the general timidity of conservatives, we would assume that the same relationship between conservatism and talking politics is also true here. One clue would be to examine the voting behavior of expressive and inexpressive teachers. Those who are not expressive and do not talk about politics in class tend to be Republicans, whereas those who are expressive and do talk about politics in class are generally Democrats. Republicans and conservatives participate less in politics both inside and outside of the classroom than Democrats and liberals. Among the general population the reverse is true. Although the Democratic party has the majority of registered voters, the Republican party normally turns out its supporters in greater force. However, this is largely an artifact of the class composition of the Democratic and Republican parties. The Democratic party draws its greatest strength from among low-income groups, hence we can expect a smaller turnout for the Democratic candidates. Among the better educated middle- to high-income groups, Democratic participation is probably greater than Republican participation. Teachers, as members of the middle-income population group, probably reflect the normal pattern of behavior.

Given the fact that the expressive, talkative teachers are Democrats, what can we say about the types of schools most likely to generate political interest among students in the class? In the first place, we know that politics in the classroom tends to be an urban rather than a rural phenomenon. There is a distinct difference in the expressive behavior of big-city teachers compared to small-town teachers. Big-city teachers talk politics more often in class and tend to be liberal; small-town teachers do not talk about politics very much in class and tend to be conservative. Incidentally, although small-town teachers are less expressive generally, they are more likely to prefer the expression of conservative than liberal opinions. This is especially true of small-town teachers who were raised in a small town.

The small-town environment is simply not a political environment. Nobody talks very much about politics, but when they do they tend to be conservative. The greater expressivism of small-town conservatives as compared with small-town liberals is an exception to the general rule. Actually, since so little political discussion goes on in small-town schools, the over-all significance of this deviant pattern is minimal. As far as small-town teachers themselves are concerned, the environment certainly is not conducive to the enjoyment of political debate.

The sharp differences between metropolitan schools and small-town schools may help us to understand why people in large cities are generally affiliative and active in politics. Perhaps the socializing function of the small-town school is to minimize the significance of politics, or the school may simply be reflecting the nonpolitical environment of the small town in which it exists. If nobody in the community cares much about politics, the schools are not likely to exhibit any great interest. At any rate, the schools and the community seem to perform complementary functions.

Politics is discussed most often in the social studies because of the relevant nature of the subject matter. This is indeed the case. About 80 per cent of the social studies instructors spend much time talking about politics with their classes. No other discipline comes anywhere near this total. For instance, only about 15 per cent of the English and foreign language teachers indicate that they discuss politics in class very much.

However important the intensity of political discussion is, we are still interested in the total amount of discussion that takes place. For instance, a teacher might talk about politics only once or twice in an entire year, but his discussions might be so useful or controversial that they excite the students toward political thinking and, perhaps, even political participation. A single really interesting discussion in class might prove to be highly significant. If we include those teachers who *occasionally* talk about politics in class, then political discussion does not seem to be so rare. Ninety per cent of the social studies instructors talk about politics in class; 62 per cent of the English and foreign language teachers do; about 41 per cent of agriculture, physical education, general education, and business education teachers; about 39 per cent of mathematics and science teachers; about 34 per cent of art and music teachers.

This ranking is akin to the ranking of courses according to expressive behavior orientations and ideology. Table IV shows that the social studies teachers, English, and foreign language teachers are the most expressive teachers, and that their expressive orientations are carried over into the classroom situation. Notice that there is a clear relationship between political ideology, talking politics in class, and expressive orientations. The social studies, English, and foreign languages are populated by liberal teachers who talk a lot

TABLE IV: ROLE ORIENTATION, TALKING POLITICS
IN CLASS, AND IDEOLOGY (in ranks)

Role Perception*	Talking Politics in Class**	Ideology***
1. Social studies (52)	1 (97)	1 (49)
2. English, foreign language (48)	2 (63)	2 (39)
3. Art, music (41)	6 (34)	3 (36)
4. Math, science (40)	5 (39)	4 (29)
5. Agriculture, physical education, home economics (37)	4 (40)	6 (23)
6. Business and general education (36)	3 (42)	5 (27)

r (Kendall's w) = .74

* Mean expressive response to all items.
** Percentage indicating they "always," "often," or "sometimes" talk about politics in class.
*** Per cent liberal.

about politics in class, and who think that this is the proper sort of thing for them to do. Teachers of business and general education have low perceptions of their expressive roles, do not talk about politics in class very much, and are rather conservative.

FACTS AND VALUES: IS THERE A DISTINCTION?

Liberals talk more about politics in class, but this does not necessarily mean that they express personal points of view, but they probably do. It is difficult for a teacher to conceal personal values. For high school teachers the distinction between facts and values is very obscure.

Given the opportunity to judge a variety of statements expressing the basic "truths" of either the liberal or the conservative faiths, teachers were unable to decide whether a statement was a fact or a value. A substantial proportion of the teachers declared the following statement to be a fact: "The American form of government may not be perfect, but it is the best type of government yet devised by man." This statement is of the chauvinistic variety which Litt maintains is not prevalent in textbooks. Many high school teachers believe it to be an empirical truth that America has the best type of government yet devised by man. Even though the statement includes the word *best,* 42 per cent of the teachers called the statement factual. Philosophers of science would tell us that the inclusion of an evaluative word automatically makes the statement ineligible for empirical verification and, therefore, not factual. But schools of education do not strongly emphasize logic. Fifty per cent of the teachers said that it was an opinion that could be expressed in class; only 3 per cent maintained that one should not express this opinion in class. If teachers believe that children can be told that ours is the most perfect form of government yet devised by man, it is no wonder that freshmen receive a rather severe shock when they are told by college professors that the Founding Fathers wrote the Constitution partially as a conservative reaction to the excesses of revolutionary democracy.

What kinds of teachers are most likely to think that the statement about the quality of the American government is a fact? Those who agree with it (conservatives): 55 per cent of those teachers who strongly agree with this statement call it a fact, as did 25 per cent of those who agree with it but not quite so strongly. None of the few teachers who disagreed with this statement thought it to be factual. The general rule is that the stronger the agreement with the values expressed in a statement, the stronger the inclination to regard the statement as one of fact. More conservatives than liberals agree with the statement, and consequently are more inclined to describe it as factual, the difference between the two ideological positions becomes most pronounced in small towns, where one third of the liberals but one half of the conservatives thought the statement one of fact. The small-town conservative teacher, then, is a true embodiment of what critics of the public schools call good old-fashioned patriotism. Males, who are more liberal than females, are also more likely to think the statement factual than females are. The tendency of males to regard the statement as one of fact is especially great among the more experienced teachers. About 33 per cent of the inexperienced teachers consider the statement to be a fact, but 57 per cent of the experienced males and 49 per cent of the experienced females did, further evidence that the teaching experience operates to strengthen the values of conformity. Teachers who genuinely believe that ours is the best of all possible worlds are not likely to encourage their students to be critical of the system.

We noted earlier that social studies teachers tend to be liberal. Readers who are disturbed by this may be reassured to know that the majority of social studies teachers also think that the American government is the world's greatest, and that social studies teachers are the most likely to produce uncritical acceptance of the system among high school students.

Some further evidence of the rather harmless nature of the relationship between liberalism and talking politics in class lies in the relationship between political participation and belief in the sanctity of American government. Those most active in the political process are likely to have strong convictions; in the most active these beliefs should become so strongly held that the distinction between facts and values becomes obscured. Just as political participation induces strong partisanship in the political process, it should also produce strong adherence to values. This expectation is clearly supported by the response to the statement about American government. One third of the teachers who are not active in the political process but a majority of those who are active think the statement is one of fact. One half of the teachers who are extremely interested in politics think it is factual, but only one fourth of those who indicate that their interest in politics is not very great do. The same relationship between activity and belief in the factual nature of the statement holds for classroom behavior: 56 per cent of those who often talk about politics in class but only 40 per cent of those who never talk about politics in class say the statement is a fact.

SUMMARY

Teachers make a clear distinction between intraclass and extraclass behavior. Certain activities which thought proper outside the classroom are improper in it. This distinction applies not only to role perception, but also to actual behavior. Teachers are more likely to talk about politics with family and friends than with their classes. Conservative teachers are less expressive in their orientations and behavior than are liberal teachers; however, conservative teachers are not as frightened of the classroom as are liberal teachers. This means that liberals are likelier to talk about politics in class in spite of the risk of sanctions. However, liberals are also more likely to emphasize chauvinistic evaluations of American government.

Teachers who are active in the political process are expressive in their approach to the classroom; teachers who are active in educational associations are quiescent in their classroom role orientations. Politics is talked about most often in social studies classes, and especially in metropolitan areas. In small towns political discussion in the classroom is practically nonexistent. Most teachers are conservative, and conservatives are not inclined to disclose personal opinions. The greater tendency of liberals to express themselves counteracts the conservative dominance of the teaching profession to some extent. However, there is no evidence that either liberals or conservatives are anxious to encourage students to undertake critical evaluation of American institutions. The educational association squelches criticism, and teachers who are heavily involved in association activities are relatively uncritical.

The classroom operates basically to reinforce a belief in the desirability of maintaining the *status quo*. It is very doubtful that the classroom experience of students encourages them toward radical politics. If there is brain washing in the high schools, it is clearly not for indoctrination in socialism; rather, it appears aimed at the production of optimistic, uncritical citizens. The political world of the high schools is not the world of the politicians.

Chapter Five:
SANCTIONS
AND
THE ROOTS OF FEAR

The school is under constant pressure from the community it serves; in some periods the pressure is more intense than in others, but it never really dies down. In the early and mid-1950's when the late Senator McCarthy was riding the crest of a wave of hysteria about alleged domestic communist conspiracies, the contagion spread quickly to the public schools. Taking advantage of this outbreak of fear, experienced right wing leaders distributed vast amounts of literature claiming that most teachers and textbooks were advocates of socialism. A substantial number of public school teachers were fired, many of them summarily on the basis of unsubstantiated and frequently anonymous accusations of disloyalty. In some cases the Federal Bureau of Investigation supplied school boards with evidence of subversive activities on the part of teachers, and some state governments established their own investigating apparatus. In 1954, the *Denver Post* reported that FBI agents frequently went directly to school board officials with information relating to the loyalty of teachers.

School administrators occasionally encouraged teachers who had been anonymously accused of subversion to resign. More often, however, teachers quit of their own accord rather than face constant harassment.

The excesses of the era crept into every corner of the nation, touching public and private schools everywhere. In Englewood, N.J., Battle Creek, Mich., Pasadena, Cal., Denver, Col., Eugene, Ore., and New York City, attacks upon public schools and teachers gradually mounted to almost ferocious intensity. Neither school administrators nor professional associations mounted any very vigorous counterattack but the immoderations of the McCarthy years gradually ebbed of their own accord.

Since then the educational scene has been calm, except for an occasional incident. In 1961, for example, the Texas House of Representatives passed a resolution urging that "the American history courses in the public schools emphasize . . . our glowing and throbbing history of hearts and souls inspired by wonderful American principles and traditions. . . ." [1] In view of the findings of the last chapters, such a resolution was probably superfluous. Nevertheless, it indicates the constant concern of the community for its schools. In Fullerton, Cal., the NEA found that the community's zeal to keep its children free of subversive tendencies had created a substantial morale problem among the public school teachers. The NEA report commented that:

> It is clear from teacher testimony that most teachers in the district feel restrained not to join any community organization which represents minority viewpoints or is considered controversial, extremely liberal, or extremely conservative . . . Some division heads, principals, and in one instance the president of the faculty club, have cautioned teachers to be careful in making statements on controversial subjects in their classrooms which might be misinterpreted. It is evident that the teachers in this district feel an unusual degree of restraint and do not enjoy freedom of inquiry and communication. This is particularly true in the social sciences, English, and health education areas and is attributed primarily to community attacks upon the schools and individual teachers.[2]

The intensity of efforts to control what goes on in the schools varies from one community to another. However, the entrance of the John Birch Society into the school-criticism business has brought an element of national coordination of local criticisms of the public schools. The Parent-Teacher Association, which the Birch Society has often attacked and in some instances tried to infiltrate, maintains that the pressures on public schools are as severe now as in the days of McCarthy. Whether or not the PTA is correct, the essential

---

[1] Quoted in Jack Nelson and Gene Roberts, Jr., *The Censors and the Schools* (Boston: Little, Brown & Co., 1963), p. 134.

[2] *Fullerton, California: Report of an Investigation* (California Teachers' Association and National Education Association, May 1961), p. 15.

point is that the McCarthy era was simply an extreme manifestation of a chronic situation. Because they deal with children, schools will always be the center of public controversy.

Teachers themselves, as the people who have the most-sustained contact with the children, naturally bear the brunt of the attacks. Actually, a great deal of the antischool literature is aimed at the purportedly subversive nature of textbooks rather than at teachers. Raywid's investigation of organizations concerning themselves with public schools indicates that teachers themselves, despite their centrality in the educational institution, are not favorite targets.[3] Nevertheless, a majority of the organizations responding to Raywid's questionnaire indicated that they were concerned with the attitudes, beliefs, and patriotism of teachers.

It may be that the critics of the schools focus upon broad educational targets (ranging all the way from John Dewey's educational philosophy to sex education), teachers are nonetheless vulnerable to attack. Gross discovered that Massachusetts school administrators received numerous demands and protests relating to the views of teachers.[4] Of fifteen possible types of demand made upon school administrators and school board members, one of the more frequently mentioned related to the values and ideologies of teachers. Most of the demands that come to the attention of administrators concern money. Excluding money matters, only demands involving the nature of the curriculum and athletic programs exceeded the number of protests about the views expressed by teachers.

We have a picture, then, of teachers being constrained and harassed by the community. Is this a true picture? Is it really true that teachers regard themselves as being under community pressure, or is it perhaps the case that the most-frequently quoted spokesmen for public education have exaggerated the intensity of community pressure because of their own natural inclinations to play it safe? Are teachers bullied by patriotic groups, or is the menace of the Radical Right more of a threat to administrators than to teachers?

We are concerned here with teachers' perceptions of probable sanctions, not the existence of actual sanctions. However, teachers

[3] Mary Anne Raywid, *The Ax-Grinders* (New York: The Macmillan Co., 1962), p. 7.

[4] Neal Gross, *Who Runs Our Schools?* (New York: John Wiley and Sons, Inc., 1958), p. 50.

are in a position to know what frightens them. Their perceptions of the real world might be correct, but the distinction between the perceptual world and the real world is never very clear. As W. I. Thomas explains, "if men define situations as real, they are real in their consequences." [5] Merton's idea of the self-fulfilling prophecy illustrates the blurring of the distinctions between perceptions and reality: if a drunk in a bar becomes belligerent because he believes everyone is trying to beat him up, he may actually hit someone in self-defense and thus create the situation he feared.[6] Southern politicians who regularly predict that any effort toward integration will result in mass violence are hoping that the self-fulfilling prophecy will work for them. At any rate, the point is clear that an important clue to the understanding of an individual's behavior is his perception of the world. Thus, teachers' perceptions of sanctions can be taken as descriptions of *their* world.

By sanctions, I mean *any sort of behavior undertaken by an individual or group that is designed to deter or inhibit a potential act by a teacher.* I make no distinction between illegitimate sanctions and legitimate sanctions. From an evaluative point of view, one could argue that any sanction imposed upon a teacher for the expression of an opinion or the performance of an act is illegitimate, for, in a democratic society political behavior should not be blocked by negative sanctions. From this point of view, it makes no difference whether or not the sanction is a legitimate one (for example, asking for equal time to debate a teacher about a statement concerning public policy) or illegitimate one (making anonymous accusations against the teacher). The threat of either type of sanction might be to inhibit expressive behavior, and any inhibition of expressive behavior can be taken to be unhealthy for a democratic society.

A distinction can be made relative to the severity of sanctions which might be imposed upon a teacher. Presumably, the severity of sanctions varies both with the type of behavior which a teacher might undertake and with the source from which the sanction

---

[5] Cited in Robert Merton, "The Self-Fulfilling Prophecy" in Robert Merton, *Social Theory and Social Structure* (New York: The Free Press of Glencoe, Inc., 1957), p. 421.

[6] *Ibid.,* p. 421-436.

originates. For example, if a teacher became a precinct worker during an election, his principal might do no more than offer mild chastisement, while the superintendent might be a bit more severe in his criticism. However, if the same teacher became active in a union, both the principal and the superintendent could be expected to impose sterner punishments.

The severity of sanctions might also vary with the extent to which the values of teachers are in harmony with the community. If there is a clear and consistent difference between teachers' values and the community's values, then teachers might not be serving the function of transmitters of cultural norms, and might be perceived by the community to be operating as instigators of social change. If they are thus perceived, the number and severity of sanctions might be increased substantially, if it is true that most sanctions do originate from the community. But if most sanctions originate from within the educational system, then any discrepancy between teachers' values and the community's values would not be so important.

I do not believe that teachers look upon the community itself as a source of sanctions. Rather, they see themselves as more consistently and more severely threatened from within the educational system; more specifically, teachers are more threatened by the conservatism of the educational establishment than by the conservatism of the community. But inasmuch as teachers themselves lean toward conservatism, the conservative pressure upon them is probably reinforcing rather than inhibiting. That is to say, teachers are probably not likely to try to change the *status quo,* and the threat of sanctions guarantees that they will not try.

TEACHER VALUES AND COMMUNITY VALUES

In support of these arguments, let us first compare teacher values and community values. With regard to educational philosophy, teachers in large and small communities alike are more progressive than the community. Within the community itself, there is a substantial feeling of hostility about the way the schools are doing their jobs.[7] Almost half of the population believes that public schools are

---

[7] These statements about the attitudes of citizens are derived from data on Oregon communities provided by Professor Robert E. Agger of the University of Oregon.

not giving enough emphasis to fundamentals and that they put too much emphasis on cooperation, not enough on competition. About one fourth of the population believes that schools change pupils too far away from their parents' ideas. Few teachers subscribe to either of these beliefs; most teachers accept the dogmas of educational progressivism uncritically. In the general population there is a strong current of distrust of modern education. The disparity in the values placed respectively by the community and by teachers on progressive education may provide a clue to the nature of the sanctioning activity which community members typically introduce. Demands that the curriculum be revised to emphasize the traditional three R's are heard far more frequently than any other demand. The return to fundamentals is a basic tenet underlying almost every criticism of public education, those that emanate from the more scholarly critics of education as much as the less articulate myriad that have sprung up to find out why Johnny can't read.

On questions of educational philosophy it is a clear case of the schools versus the community: teachers are progressive, the community is not. We can assume that the community itself is the originator of most sanctions concerning the academic nature of the curriculum. However, a comparison of community and teacher values on questions of political philosophy does not produce such a sharp confrontation. As we already know, big-city teachers are more liberal than small-town teachers, but are small-town teachers conservative *because* they teach in small towns and are big-city teachers liberal *because* they teach in big cities? The normal assumption would be that this is correct—we are used to describing the small town as the bedrock of conservatism in America. It seems at least possible that teachers simply reflect the dominant ideologies prevailing in the communities where they teach.

However, this is not really the case, for small-town people are not quite as conservative as the tradition has it nor urban dwellers quite so liberal. This means, in effect, that big-city teachers are somewhat more liberal than their community and small-town teachers are somewhat more conservative than their community.

Given the opportunity to agree or disagree with the statement "The government ought to help people to get doctors and hospital care at low cost," roughly the same proportion of community residents and teachers in large cities agreed. However, in small towns 40 per cent of the teachers as compared to 59 per cent of the residents agreed. In response to the statement "The government in Washington ought to see to it that everybody who wants to work can find a job," both city teachers and city residents agreed once again at the same rate. In small towns, in contrast one-third and 52 per cent of the residents agreed. On these questions, the community appears to be significantly more liberal than the teachers in the smaller towns. On questions of federal aid to education teachers everywhere are substantially more liberal than the community, but it is only on this latter issue, which directly relates to education, that small town teachers are more liberal than the community.

If small-town teachers are more conservative than their community and big-city teachers are less conservative than their community, does this mean that sanctions should be less severe in the smaller towns? It is difficult to say. There is the effect of the *disparity* of differences to be considered. On the response to the propositions, the difference between teachers' values and community values is very slight in the cities, but is substantial in the small towns. There is also the matter of the direction of difference. The disparity between teacher values and community values in the large cities is just the reverse of this disparity in small towns. Although there is a larger difference between the values of small-town teachers and those of their community, the teachers lean somewhat to the right. Since most pressures from the community originate from the right wing of the ideological spectrum, the direction of the disparity might mean that small-town teachers are less subject to sanction.

Does the greater disparity in small towns mean that teachers there are more likely to be sanctioned than city teachers are? Or does the direction of the difference, the magnitude aside, mean that small-town teachers are rather safe from community pressures? There is, in fact, no appreciable difference between the perceptions of big-city and small-town teachers with regard to sanctions. The traditional assumption that small towns are more difficult to teach in because of the relatively exposed position of the school does not seem to explain the attitudes of small-town teachers. Had the disparity between teachers and community been great and had teachers been leaning to the left of the community, perceptions of sanctions in small towns might have been increased.

But it may be that the community itself is not very important as a source of pressure upon the behavior and attitudes of teachers after all. Small towns are supposed to be more threatening than large cities, but teachers there do not appear to be especially intimidated although the fact that small-town teachers are generally less politically oriented than are their big-city counterparts should make them *less* fearful of sanctions than teachers in large cities, if the community is perceived as a sanctioning agent.

WHOM DO TEACHERS FEAR?

Who do teachers believe would threaten them if they undertook controversial courses of action? To arrive at some estimate of their perceptual world, teachers were asked to evaluate the probable reaction of given groups and individuals to the teacher actions of going on strike, explaining to their class their preference of Presidential candidate, speaking in class in favor of socialism, allowing an atheist to address the class, taking part in CORE or NAACP demonstrations, speaking in class against the John Birch Society, speaking in class in favor of Medicare, and speaking in class in favor of the United Nations.

Teachers were asked, first, to evaluate whether or not a given group or individual would approve or disapprove of a given action; second, if the reactions were disapproval to guess what sort of retaliatory or punitive gesture could be expected. The catalog of sanctioning activities included very moderate (wanting to present the other side, disagreeing publicly, and so forth) to very extreme (demanding public investigations or pressuring the administration to fire the teacher). The teachers ranked the individuals and the groups from most to least threatening with the following result:

1. Local cranks;
2. Parents;
3. Members of the school board;
4. Superintendents;
5. Principals;

6. Other teachers;
7. Patriotic groups;
8. Church or religious groups;
9. Republican politicians;
10. Students;
11. Newspapers;
12. Business groups;
13. Tax opposition groups;
14. Veterans groups;
15. Democratic politicians;
16. City officials;
17. Farm organizations; and
18. Labor unions.

This ranking makes it clear that teachers perceive sanctions as originating from within the educational system rather than from within the community. Except for the local cranks, people who habitually harass the educational system, the agents which teachers perceive as potential sanctioners are parents, school board members, superintendents, principals, and other teachers. Students are the only intraschool group missing from the top third of the list of sanctioners.

One might want to argue that these perceptions are not reality, which is of course true. The fact that teachers are, in effect, buffered from the community by the administration might cause them to look upon the administration as a direct source of sanctions, whereas in reality the administration might merely be transmitting sanctions originating within the community. There is no immediate rebuttal to this argument. However, Gross' study of administrators in Massachusetts indicates that they, too, see the greatest source of pressure as originating from within the school system.[8] Superintendents and school board members indicated that the greatest pressure upon them came from parents, school board members, and teachers. Guessing what forms sanctions might take, teachers were free to indicate that a sanction would flow to the administration rather than directly to them, but very few did this. In most cases, moreover, the administration was perceived as the originator rather than the transmitter

[8] Gross, *op. cit.*

of the threat; indeed teachers did not regard administrators as defenders against community pressures.

THE THREAT OF THE INTRASCHOOL ENVIRONMENT

Keeping in mind that these responses are measures not of actual events but of probable events, it appears that the participants in the educational system—the societal subsystem charged with the duty of transmitting cultural norms—do not look upon the community as a source of severe danger. Contrast this perception with the description of attacks upon the schools by patriotic groups that are said to exert unremitting pressure against the school system. At practically every convention attended by school administrators or other educationists, a panel discussion of pressure groups and the schools is a standard event. Yet to the teachers themselves, so-called pressure groups are a small threat compared to parents, superintendents, school board members, and principals.

For example, teachers believe that should they strike to secure higher salaries and benefits, the school board, and the superintendent would impose maximum sanctions that would, in essence, end their teaching careers. On the other hand, patriotic groups are perceived as objecting to strike action, but not in so severe a fashion. No matter what the issue, even if it is criticizing the John Birch Society or speaking in favor of socialism, the threat of the patriotic groups does not appear to teachers to be as great as the threat from parents or school administrators. This means that teachers are not especially frightened of the Birch Society and comparable organizations. No matter how much noise these organizations make, they run poor second to parents and school administrators as potential inhibitors of teacher behavior.

The exceedingly repressive perception of administrators can be explained to some extent by the fact that school administrators generally are very cautious, anxious to avoid clashes with the community. They may let it be known to the teaching staff, in a subtle fashion, that the successful teacher is the cautious teacher. The principal is an exception to these generalizations. He ranks very high on the list of potential sanctioning agents, but teachers believe that principals are likely to be relatively mild sanctioners, less severe than other teachers as a matter of fact. Principals sanction on as many or more issues than the other high ranking sanctioners, but in a very mild fashion. The other sanctioners of high rank are perceived as being considerably more tenacious and severe. Students are perceived to be more vicious in their sanctions than principals.

The teacher perception of the principal that emerges seems to be one of a benevolent authority—the principal will undertake punitive action in the same fashion that a father would discipline a mischievous child. The principal is accepted as the supreme authority in the school, but his basic function is to support, not sanction, the teacher, especially in cases of parental interference. But being an agent of support, the principal has a powerful sanction weapon: refusal to support a teacher in critical situations. His most effective sanction may simply be to do nothing. As the administrative officer for the school, the principal has at his disposal other relatively undramatic but nevertheless quite effective sanctioning techniques. He has the authority to distribute unpleasant extra duties among his teachers. He also controls the use of various equipment and the assigning of rooms. Some rooms have better lights than others; certain equipment never works properly. The principal's control over such trivial affairs can be a very basic resource for sanctions. The following comment, as reported by Becker, illustrates this point. A teacher was asked what might happen if she disobeyed a principal. The teacher replied:

> There were lots of things she could do. She had charge of assigning children to their new rooms when they passed. If she didn't like you she could really make it tough for you. You'd get all the slow children and all the behavior problems, the dregs of the school. After six months of that, you really know what work meant. She had methods like that.[9]

Since the principal controls the day-to-day life of the teacher, the sanctions which he can impose are more annoying than dangerous, but administered in a cumulative manner they can be quite effective.

The principal is not likely to kick up much of a public fuss, but a

---

[9] Howard S. Becker, "The Teacher in the Authority System of the Public School," *Journal of Educational Sociology*, 27 (November 1953), p. 138.

superintendent lacking recourse to the principal's resources, might. Part of the conflict between teachers and administrators is attributable to their differing role perceptions of the proper role of the teacher. Administrators tend to look upon teachers as serving a liaison role between school and community whereas teachers regard themselves as transmitters of basic societal norms to children. Thus, principals and superintendents are delighted when teachers take an active role in accepted community affairs in order to enhance the "just folks" image which administrators find so beneficial. Teachers who become Cub Scout den mothers or address Rotary Clubs may find themselves in excellent rooms teaching bright children.

Some conflict between teachers and administrators is inevitable because of the different demands of the position that each occupies, but such conflict is mild compared to the conflict of parents with teachers. Waller has called parents and teachers "natural enemies." [10] Although they both have the interest of the child at heart, the fundamental conflict between parents and teachers occurs because each has a legitimate yet competing claim for the child's obedience. The teacher can lay claim to a special competence built by professional training. The parent has no such competence and, according to the teacher, cannot thoroughly understand the problems of education. Therefore, parents are considered to have no legitimate right to interfere with schoolwork.

Because they do have a legitimate claim for authority over their child, parents are likely to challenge the teacher. The challenge of parents becomes especially crucial because the classroom authority of the teacher is already slipping. Thus, the basic fear that teachers have of parents stems from two sources: first, they resent nonprofessional advice on how to do their jobs; second and more important, they fear that an intrusion by the parents will damage their authority position. The ideal world for the teacher would be a world without parents. Failing this, the next most desirable alternative is active participation by parents in the PTA. It has been found that parents who take an active role in the PTA are more likely to approve of new teaching techniques than are parents who are not members. Participation in the PTA increases the identification

---

[10] Willard Waller, *The Sociology of Teaching* (New York: John Wiley and Sons, Inc., 1965), p. 68.

of the parent with the school and reduces the antagonism toward the teacher. At the same time, participation makes the parent more of an insider in school matters and thus reduces the antagonism of the teacher. Thus, active PTA participants have substantially greater positive attitudes toward schools than do nonmembers.

The nonprofessional aspects of the parent-teacher relationship are also present in the perceptions of school board members by teachers. School board members, like parents, are representative of the lay community. Like parents, they are more threatening than either the superintendent or the principal, both of whom symbolize the professional system. The potential control of the lay community might be described as even more illegitimate than that of parents, since it originates more obviously from outsiders. As outsiders, they do not necessarily share the norms of the educational establishment. Lay school boards are less likely to be educationally progressive than are principals or superintendents. Hence, the demand for a return to the three R's could easily originate from a school board, but would probably not originate from professional administrators.

There are almost no reciprocal sanctions that teachers can impose on teachers, school board members, superintendents, or parents. Teachers can sanction their principal, however. Becker points out that if enough teachers request transfers to another school in the system, the attention of higher authorities will focus upon the principal. In some cases, teachers may use their connections in the community to create antagonism toward the principal. None of these possibilities really exists with regard to the school board, superintendent, or the parents. The principal is, in a sense, the weakest of all the sanctioning agents whose positions are superior to that of the teachers. As Becker says:

> Both parties to the conflict have at their disposal effective means of controlling the other's behavior, so that the ordinary situation is one of compromise (if there is a dispute at all), with sanctions being used only when the agreed on boundaries are over-stepped.[11]

Since parents and school boards do not interact this intensely with teachers, the establishment of a set of rules is more difficult.

[11] Becker, *op. cit.*, p. 139.

There is a curiously ambivalent perception of teachers with regard to students in comparison to principals. Principals have legitimate authority over teachers, teachers have legitimate authority over students. Yet, in spite of the formal chain of command, students are more severe sanctioners than principals. Students are their technical subordinates, but they have some very effective means of controlling the behavior of teachers. The most powerful resource of students is, of course, their parents to whom they can report their classroom experiences.

Colleagues, whose position is one of peer rather than one of subordinate or superordinate are another source of possible sanctions for teachers. Presumably, teachers should be expected to cooperate with one another and to defend themselves against attacks from outsiders, whether these outsiders be superintendents or parents. Teachers should be expected to avoid directly endangering one another's authority. Most of these rules of conduct deal with the problem, as expected, of authority. Teachers are not supposed to disagree with one another in front of their pupils, for example. But according to teachers, their colleagues can be rather difficult to get along with. If teachers were to go on strike, or to express personal preferences for a Presidential candidate, or to speak in favor of socialism or to allow an atheist to address the class, or take part in racial demonstrations, they believe their colleagues would not only disapprove but would do something about it. Thus, the relative quiescence of teachers is not only imposed upon them from above by the members of the school board and the superintendent, it is also established by means of peer group norms. All groups establish norms and punish deviants. The group norm of teachers, as they describe it, is the avoidance of controversy.

Consider, for example, the question of going on strike. Here the teachers themselves are more threatening than is the principal. One source of the difficulty in organizing teachers into unions might be not only the fact that most people do not believe teachers should take part in such activity, but also that the norms of the teaching profession itself forbid it. Public opposition to strikes among teachers is admittedly severe. In Utah, public school teachers held a two-day meeting in 1964 during school time, to discuss possible methods of raising salaries. Although the teachers made it clear they intended to return to their classroom at the end of this period, the public regarded their action as a strike, and disapproved rather severely. The two-day meeting created some negative reaction against the teachers, especially among Republicans and upper-income groups. Granted that public reaction to teacher walkouts is negative, it is probably not much more negative than it is about strikes in general. But unions continue to authorize strikes despite substantial public disapproval. The greatest roadblock in the way of union efforts to organize teachers is, not public disapproval, but the attitudes of the teachers themselves.

Teachers also impose negative group norms on the matter of taking part in NAACP or CORE demonstrations. Whereas taking part in such demonstrations is less central to the professional image of the teacher than is going on strike, teachers still define this activity as illegitimate. Perhaps the fact that such demonstrations are usually identified by the community as radically innovative contributes to the teachers' negative attitude toward them. Yet, as is true with regard to strikes, a more likely explanation is that the group norms of teachers simply forbid any sort of deviant behavior. In this teachers are more conservative than their students, who find nothing objectionable in this kind of behavior, to which parents and school administrators could be expected to react rather sharply to racial demonstrations on the part of teachers.

THREATS FROM THE COMMUNITY

Among the extraschool sanctioning agents, local cranks, patriotic groups, newspapers, church or religious groups, and Republican politicians seem to be the most consistently threatening. The other agents, although occasionally severe in their perceived sanctions, generally get exercised only by one or two periodically recurrent issues. Hence, tax-opposition groups become annoyed by strikes; business organizations would be upset by a teacher's use of the classroom as a forum to express a preference of Presidential candidate. Veterans groups become angry at utterances in favor of socialism; and so on.

Local cranks are a small cadre of people who regularly seize upon the school as an example of the evils of the community, but are not identified with any organization. Among organizations, patriotic groups are the most threatening. Although they would sanction on few issues, the perceived extremity of their sanctioning activity is exceeded only by that perceived of parents and members of the school board. Patriotic groups do not get so upset over the issue of striking as do the intraschool groups; their greatest anxiety is attracted by the possibility that a teacher might allow an atheist to address a class, or might speak in favor of socialism and against the John Birch Society.

Teachers believe that patriotic organizations have probably defined teacher values as liberal. We have seen that patriotic groups typically define teachers as agents of socialism. It appears, therefore, that even though teachers themselves are inclined somewhat toward the conservative end of the political spectrum, they see the threats of the community originating primarily from conservative groups. Of course, the perception of the teachers may be faulty, but this is not the point. One example of faulty teachers' perception may be the low-threat ranking given to tax-opposition groups. This ranking contrasts with Gross's study of administrators, who ranked taxpayers' associations as very highly threatening. Administrators are more directly concerned with the financial aspects of school operations and could be expected to be more attuned to a potential revolt of the taxpayers. Most studies of school finance indicate that taxpayers' organizations vigorously oppose increases in school expenditures. For teachers, however, these pressures do not amount to very much because they do not interact with such groups regularly, as do administrators.

Perception of sanctions is to some extent a function of one's position within an organization. Nevertheless, an examination of the perceived reaction of the various extraschool sanctioning agents provides us with some interesting examples of the teacher's view of the community. For example, church or religious groups are perceived as very conservative, potentially as rough as patriotic groups on some issues. Churches have not been nearly so quick to condemn teachers as patriotic groups have been, but they rank high among the forces of conservatism. On the question of socialism, other perceived sanctioners are newspapers and veterans' groups, but business groups, which one would assume to feel a direct stake in the perpetuation of capitalism, are defined as less threatening than newspapers, and newspapers emerge as a much more conservative force within the community than we would expect, judging from descriptions community pressures supplied by educational associations.

Interesting comparison can be made between perceptions of Democratic and Republican politicians. Democratic politicians are relatively harmless. Only if one spoke in favor of a Presidential candidate would they sanction. However, Republican politicians, in addition to being reluctant to have the classroom become a forum for the expression of teacher preferences about elections, would also sanction on specific matters of public policy such as teacher strikes and speaking in favor of socialism. In other words, Democrats are viewed essentially as having no objections to most of the activities, even strikes, which teachers might want to undertake, whereas Republicans are more concerned with both the content of teaching and the behavior of teachers. Hence their substantially higher rank than Democrats on the list of potential sanctioners.

The greater threat perceived from the Republicans is reflective of a very substantial consensus among teachers, the majority of whom are Republicans. If we look at a differential ranking of Democratic and Republican teachers, both Democrats and Republicans among the teaching population are more afraid of Republican politicians than they are of Democratic politicians, and Republican teachers are, therefore, more afraid of Republican politicians than are Democratic teachers.

The consensus among teachers with regard to the relative threats of the Democratic and the Republican parties is an interesting attestation to the images of both major parties in view of the fact that teacher perceptions generally follow ideological lines. That is to say, the view that a teacher has of a given group is to some extent a function of the values which the teacher holds. For example, liberals are much more frightened of patriotic groups than are conservatives. We may assume, therefore, that the negative reaction to the Republican party is not so much a consequence of possible perceptual distortion of teachers as it is one of the actual behavior of the Republican party in school politics. There is a growing body of literature which suggests that, although the national images of the major parties are the Democrats as liberals and the Republicans as conservatives, in local matters the reverse is frequently the case.

It has been found that Republican voters more frequently support the expenditure of local funds for community improvement than do Democrats; higher-income Republican voters, for example, are more likely to support bond issues for the improvement of schools than are Democrats. Nevertheless, Republicans appear to be more repressive of teachers' expressions of opinion than are Democrats.

Some other comparisons of the differing perceptions of various groups of teachers are worthy of mention. We have noted that students are perceived as essentially conservative by teachers. Yet conservative teachers are much more frightened of students than are liberals; this is especially true of the small-town conservatives. The greater fear that conservative teachers have of students is somewhat related to the fact that the older teachers, who are relatively conservative look inward to the school system rather than outward to the community for sanctioning agents. For example, newer teachers rank patriotic groups considerably higher than older teachers. Thus, the inexperienced teachers perhaps reflect the standard stereotype of the community, rather than the educational system, as the greatest threat. However, as experience increases, the community ceases to be much of a problem and the educational system itself assumes greater proportions. There might be a growing realization among teachers, as they gradually redefine the situation, that parents and administrators actually are far more concerned about their behavior than is the community.

VARIATIONS IN TEACHER AWARENESS
OF SANCTIONS

Although we have talked briefly about the difference in perceptions of liberals or conservatives and Democrats or Republicans, we have made no mention of a basic dichotomy in the teaching profession. Some teachers believe that their behavior would not provoke a sanction response no matter how extreme this behavior appears. Other teachers believe that no matter how unoffending their behavior might be, the community and the educational establishment would undertake sanctioning activity. Some teachers are simply more aware of sanctions than are others. What makes a person believe that his behavior would provoke hostile responses? What makes a teacher think that no matter what sort of action is undertaken, the reaction of the community and the educational system would be immediate and unpleasant? Is concern over sanctions a result of the actual conditions surrounding the teacher? Is this concern a result of the fact that some communities really are more threatening or that some courses—social studies, for example —provoke more sanctions because of the nature of the subject matter being taught? In other words, is concern over sanctions a product of a realistic appraisal of the true state of affairs?

A teacher's reaction to the threat of sanctions is a function both of individual characteristics and of realistic appraisals of situations. To illustrate, recall that no difference was found between the respective attitudes of big-city and small-town teachers toward sanctions. However, teachers who are migrants from small-towns to large cities or from large cities to small towns are more likely to be concerned about sanctions than are teachers who live in communities of approximately the same size as those in which they were raised. In this case, the objective environment (the size of the city) does not appear to be very important, but adjustments made by the individual to that environment seem to produce a somewhat more apprehensive view of the world. That is to say, it is not living in a big or small town that makes a teacher concerned about sanctions. In short, it is not the objective environment that defines the situation, it is not the community itself that contributes to a perception of sanctions, it is the difficulty of adjusting to a community unlike the one in which the teacher was raised. Such interactions between the subjective and objective worlds are illustrated also by the different perceptions of men and women. Men are more concerned about sanctions than are women. This difference could be explained by the fact that men are considerably more aware of conflict than are women. We have noted that men are able to recall more examples of community sanctions upon teachers than women are. Men seem to be more aware of the existence of pressures than women, hence their tendency to define groups as more threatening may be realistic.

Attitudes toward sanctions also vary with mobility, a factor presumably unrelated to accurate perceptions of conflict. Upward-mobile females are much more sanction-prone than upward-mobile males, but downward-mobile males are more sanction-prone than downward-mobile females. In this case, the perception of sanctions seems to be consistent with the generally negative attitudes of downward-mobile males and upward-mobile females. We noted that mobility affects the attitudes of males and females in exactly opposite ways, so that upward mobility principally affects females whereas downward mobility seriously affects the alienation and cynicism of males particularly. Distrust of the political and social world in general probably leads to a suspicious view of educational and community groups. Alienated and cynical teachers and those who have a low trust in others are much more likely to be sanction-prone than are teachers with less jaundiced views of the world. People who are generally suspicious could not be expected to make an exception and view the community as unthreatening. Men who are dissatisfied with their jobs are much more likely to be sanction-prone; those who are satisfied are likely to be unconcerned about probable sanctions. It is possible that job dissatisfaction is somewhat related to the existence of threats. It is more likely, however, that a reaction to work life is antecedent to the perception of threats, because among women there is no relationship at all between job satisfaction and attitudes toward sanctions. Social studies teachers should be more sanction-prone than other teachers because their topic is most likely to provoke controversy, and also because they often talk about politics in class. The fact that social studies teachers are considerably more concerned about sanctions follows naturally from their actual role in the classroom.

There is an interesting contrast between the educational progressivism that dominates the educational establishment and the political conservatism that seems to be typical of those teachers who are unconcerned about community threats. Earlier it was argued that educational progressivism is the "right" posture for a teacher. If political conservatism and educational progressivism are safe, then those teachers who have both of these ideological characteristics should be free of sanctions. The consistent ideological pattern is to be liberal in politics and progressive in education, or conservative in politics and non-progressive in education. About 80 per cent of the teaching population falls into one of these consistent patterns. Their political and educational values are comparable. The remaining 20 per cent provides a very clear illustration of the damaging effects of nonconformity: nearly two-thirds of these politically liberal, educationally nonprogressive teachers are sanction-prone as compared to only one-third of those who are politically conservative but educationally progressive. The latter group is, in comparison to other kinds of teachers, practically fearless. The larger community becomes upset about political liberalism and the educational community becomes upset about educational conservatism. If a teacher can satisfy both groups, he can achieve immunity. Holding orthodox views definitely makes one feel at peace with his community.

PERCEPTIONS OF SANCTIONS AND PATTERNS OF POLITICAL ACTIVITY

What are people likely to do as a consequence of their perceptions of sanctions? Would fear of sanction deter a person from possible action, or would that fear increase his determination to proceed regardless of the consequences? Here we must make a distinction between intraclass and extraclass behavior. If it is a matter of undertaking an extraclass activity, sanction-prone teachers are more likely to believe that a given behavior is proper and should be undertaken. Sanction-prone teachers are the most likely teachers to believe that joining unions, taking part in strikes and demonstrations, criticizing local officials, and the like, are proper activities. Concern about the consequences of action does not seem to operate as a deterrent to activities undertaken outside the classroom. This relationship between propriety and perception of sanctions is probably related to the fact that the community itself is not generally regarded as a serious threat.

The classroom is the source of teachers' greatest fears, but perception of sanctions does seem to operate as a deterrent to intraclass behaviors. Whereas sanction-prone teachers see more propriety in undertaking controversial extraclass behavior, for them the classroom is not a forum for the expression of ideas. About one-half of the teachers who express no concern about sanctions are expressive in their approach to the classroom whereas only about one-third of those whose perception of potential sanctions is less optimistic are. It seems, therefore, that the classroom frightens sanction-prone teachers much more than it does teachers who do not fear sanctions. Among those teachers who see themselves as in the midst of a threatening environment, the classroom situation exaggerates the danger.

What about the actual behavior of these two kinds of teachers? The general pattern is for sanction-prone teachers to be more active both in class and in the community. Their concern about the consequences of actions does not inhibit them; rather, it seems to strengthen their willingness to express themselves. They attend political meetings, work for candidates, and in general, involve themselves in politics to a far greater extent than those teachers who are either unconcerned or unaware. Thus, the typical sanction-prone teacher is characterized by an active and critical role in the political process. The relationship between political activity and being aware of sanctions holds up even in the classroom, the source of the greatest fears of active, sanction-prone teachers. Even though they think it not quite proper to use the classroom as a forum, and even though they are acutely aware of the possible dangers of doing so, sanction-prone teachers talk about politics in class far more often than do teachers who are not aware.

The most appropriate behaviors are also the safest behaviors. Relatively few teachers are active in the class and community too, but those who are active are aware of the consequences of their activity. The nature of this relationship is correlational, not causal. It cannot be argued that teachers who are active in class and community are active *because* of their perceptions of sanctions.

CONCLUSIONS

Pressures on teachers are exaggerated by the classroom situation, possibly because it is here that the authority of the teacher is most important yet most consistently under attack. It is not the role of the teacher as citizen that is dangerous to him, it is his role as teacher. Teachers who espouse orthodox ideologies feel themselves to be relatively free of sanctions, but teachers who feel free of sanctions are not therefore more likely to use the classroom as a forum for the expression of their ideas. Rather, the reverse is true. Those teachers who are the most expressive in the classroom are more threatened by the educational establishment.

The over-all impact of perceived sanctions seems to produce docility and conformity in teachers. Men, who typically speak out more in class than women do, are more threatened than women; men do not share the ideological orthodoxy of women. The educational system does not seem to encourage outspokenness but at the same time it does not prevent speaking out. Teachers fear parents, school administrators, and school boards—those who are most directly involved in the educational process—more than they fear the community. The community is only occasionally involved in school affairs, whereas the administration and parents are constantly involved.

Schools themselves inhibit teachers more than does the community, a fact that suggests that the typical picture of the school as under constant attack from conservative-interest groups is incorrect. If teachers become less subject to intimidation, it will not be because of the weakening of the Birch Society and comparable groups. An increasing self-confidence on the part of teachers will come about if administrators and parents relax their scrutiny. If school superintendents and school boards would cease their concern for the maintenance of the *status quo,* the threat from the community would probably be of little consequence, according to the views of the teachers themselves.

INDEX